Citrus, Illustrated

For my sister Monica,
who craves my lemon curd tart

Text copyright © 2026 by George Geary.
Illustrations copyright © 2026 by Rebecca Hollingsworth.

Library of Congress Cataloging-in-Publication Data available.

ISBN 978-1-7972-3593-6

Manufactured in China.

MIX
Paper | Supporting
responsible forestry
FSC™ C008047
FSC
www.fsc.org

Design by Kelsey Cox.

10 9 8 7 6 5 4 3 2 1

Chronicle books and gifts are available at special quantity discounts
to corporations, professional associations, literacy programs, and other
organizations. For details and discount information, please contact our
premiums department at corporatesales@chroniclebooks.com or at
1-800-759-0190.

Chronicle Books LLC
680 Second Street
San Francisco, California 94107
www.chroniclebooks.com

A COOKBOOK OF
35
SWEET & SAVORY RECIPES

CITRUS, ILLUSTRATED

GEORGE GEARY

ILLUSTRATIONS BY
REBECCA
HOLLINGSWORTH

CHRONICLE BOOKS
SAN FRANCISCO

Introduction · 8

Grapefruit · 12

GRAPEFRUIT RECIPES

Kumquat · 34

KUMQUAT RECIPES

Lemon · 50

Lime · 72

Orange • 94

ORANGE RECIPES

Tangerine, Tangelo & Mandarin • 118

TANGERINE, TANGELO & MANDARIN RECIPES

Buddha's Hand & Citron · 142

BUDDHA'S HAND & CITRON RECIPES

Mixing Up Fruits: Hybrids · 158

MIXED CITRUS RECIPES

Introduction

When I was growing up, my family friends had a bountiful orange orchard. I loved the spacing of the trees and the dark green leaves. In season, the branches were heavy with bright, perfectly round, baseball-size oranges that were so sweet and juicy. Roaming around the orchard quickly became one of my favorite pastimes; to this day, those fond memories shape the way I think about the bright, tangy punch of a citrus fruit.

Fast forward to me today, living in Corona, California, dubbed the "Lemon Capital of the World," where my love for citrus blossomed even further. When I drive around downtown in early spring, the air is rich with the aroma of blossoms from rows and rows of citrus trees lining the roads. It feels akin to driving through Valencia, Spain. The humble orange—spanning cities, countries, and continents—lives on, enriching all our senses.

Citrus is not just a beautiful way to enrich simple dishes, but a practical one, too. Citrus has many applications, from the oils of the peel to the juice of the fruit. If watered and cared for correctly, citrus trees produce abundant fruit for many years. Having a tree in your yard or community garden will nourish you, bring you joy and health, and brighten darker days.

So here's a celebration of the hearty citrus plants, a less-celebrated but deeply important fruit family that has its heyday during the darkest months, its thick peel offering essential protection. Turn to this book as a guide to all things citrus—to learn about these fruits, cherish them, and put them to good use.

ON CLEANING

Wash supermarket citrus fruits with water and a fruit wash to remove any wax or residue. If using farmers' market or homegrown fruit, a simple wash with water will suffice.

ON ZESTING AND JUICING

- **Zesting:** If you plan to juice the fruit, always zest it first—it is difficult to zest the skin of a "deflated" fruit. Using a Microplane zester, hold the fruit in one hand and scrape the Microplane across the top, rotating the fruit. Avoid zesting the same spot more than once—if you get the white pith in the zest, the zest will be bitter. You may have a traditional zester, a smaller handheld tool with five sharp holes on one end that you drag over the citrus skin, creating zest strips that you must chop afterward.

- **Juicing:** Choose citrus that are heavy for their size. Roll the fruit on the counter while applying gentle pressure to soften the fruit and inside membranes to release the juice. Use a hand juicer to extract the maximum amount of juice. If you prefer less pulp, strain the juice.

- Both zest and juice can be frozen for up to 6 months. Pour the juice into ice cube trays; after freezing, place the cubes in a large plastic bag. The zest can be put into a plastic bag and frozen.

ON PREPARATION/ SECTIONING/SEGMENTING

Many citrus types can be sectioned by hand after peeling. Use a gentle touch to keep each section intact, and remove any loose white pith and strings. Other types, like lemons and limes, are cut into wedges or slices.

ON STORAGE

Store uncut citrus fruits in the fruit crisper drawer or a paper bag in the refrigerator for up to two weeks. Store cut fruits in a closed, sealed container and consume as soon as possible.

GRAPE FRUIT

Tips on Use

For preparation/sectioning: To enjoy the traditional grapefruit half at breakfast, there are grapefruit spoons with serration along the narrow tip for neatly releasing the flesh of each section from the enclosing sheath. A more readily available alternative is a small serrated knife with a narrow tip; cut all around just inside each section's sheath, then use a regular teaspoon to scoop out the flesh.

To my great dismay, grapefruits get a bad rap. Larger than most citrus varietals, with a thick pith, they are known for their slightly sweet and acidic flavor. They're some of the tangiest fruits around, and this can intimidate people—hence its underuse in most cuisines. But allow me to build a case for the punchy pink-, white-, or red-hued fruit; if you know how to harness its power, the acidic, sharp flavor profile can work beautifully in cooking and baking.

NUTRITIONAL AND HEALTH BENEFITS OF GRAPEFRUITS

Like most citrus fruits, the grapefruit is rich in vitamins and antioxidants, making it a fantastic addition to most diets, especially for staying healthy and avoiding sickness during the colder months when people gather indoors.

Grapefruits are an excellent source of:

Beta-carotene

Vitamin C

Flavanones

Lycopene

Dietary fiber

Trace amounts of potassium, calcium, and magnesium

Grapefruit can interact negatively with certain liver and blood pressure medications, so be sure to check with your doctor if you plan to start consuming more of it than you're used to.

(Rio) Red Grapefruit

(*Citrus paradisi* Macfadyen)

HISTORICAL BACKGROUND

In the early 1900s, a land developer named John H. Shary saw the potential for citrus growing in Texas's Rio Grande Valley. Shary was instrumental in arranging for the irrigation that citrus crops need, and thus, he planted over fifteen thousand acres of grapefruit orchard. He eventually became president of the Texas Citrus Fruit Growers Exchange, and his contributions to the development and scaling of the grapefruit industry earned him the name "father of the Texas citrus industry."

In 1929, farmer Arthur E. Henninger noticed a mutation in one of his grapefruit trees with a pink-flushed skin; cutting it open, he found the fruit was a deep red and noticeably sweeter. He patented the new variety Ruby Red grapefruit in 1934.

Shary promoted the new fruit by naming it after the region where it is grown, the Rio Red grapefruit. In 1993, Governor Ann Richards named Texas "Home of the Grapefruit," and January 23 was designated Texas Red Grapefruit Day.

ATTRIBUTES

Most red grapefruits are about the size of a softball, from 4¾ to 6 in [11.5 to 15 cm] in diameter. They are not as hard as an orange, with a bit of give

to the fruit. The skin is thin, smooth, and yellowish orange with faint patches of pink when ripe. The flesh is deep red, and seeds are rare. When shopping for red grapefruit, pick them up and choose those that are heavy for their size.

THE MANY USES OF RED GRAPEFRUITS

Grapefruits are generally tart compared to other citruses, but the red varieties are sweeter than other grapefruit varieties. Their juice is perfect for seafood dishes, salsas, and salads. Try segments on a cheese board with feta or goat cheese.

WHERE THEY GROW

Today, red grapefruits are cultivated in the Rio Grande area of Texas and in Florida, Arizona, California, Spain, South Africa, Turkey, Argentina, and Israel.

AVAILABILITY

Red grapefruits are available from late fall to early spring.

Pink Grapefruit

(*Citrus paradisi* Macfadyen)

HISTORICAL BACKGROUND

The pink grapefruit appeared seemingly out of nowhere one day throughout farms across America.

The real story is more intentional than that, and much longer. In 1913, on the W. B. Thompson Grove in Oneco, Florida, grove employee Samuel Collins had been picking fruit for an order when a strange pink-tinted fruit on a Marsh seedless grapefruit tree caught his eye. The tree branches were taken to Reasoner Brothers' Royal Palm Nursery, where the budwood was grafted for testing.

The same year, 8 miles away at Atwood Grove nursery, a grove supervisor named R. B. Foster also spotted a pink grapefruit, this one growing on a Walters seedless yellow-fruited tree. The nursery owner, Kimball C. Atwood, also took his branches to the Reasoner Brothers to have the budwood grafted.

More pink grapefruits were discovered—in 1920 by Archibald D. Shamel in Corona, California, and in 1953, by Carl Waibel in Texas. Eventually, the pink grapefruit became a beloved variety, celebrated nationally and stocked in produce sections across the country.

ATTRIBUTES

Pink grapefruits are round and range from 4 to 6 in [10 to 15 cm] in diameter. The skin is smooth, glossy, and thin, with a light pebbly texture that turns from green to pale yellow when ripe. Under the skin lies a thick, bitter pith protecting 10 to 14 light pink segments. They are generally seedless, though a few smaller seeds may be found. The juice is sweeter than that of a white grapefruit and less sweet than the red varieties.

THE MANY USES OF PINK GRAPEFRUITS

Pink grapefruits are valued for their medium sweetness and light pink color, which makes them versatile for chefs and home cooks. This flexible fruit is excellent for sauces, salad dressings, fruit salsas, and sweet baked dishes.

WHERE THEY GROW

Today, pink grapefruits are cultivated in Florida, Texas, and California.

AVAILABILITY

Pink grapefruits are available year-round, though they're best enjoyed winter through spring.

White Grapefruit

(Citrus paradisi Macfadyen)

HISTORICAL BACKGROUND

White grapefruits are a natural cross between an orange and a pomelo, growing on evergreen trees. The first fruits were found in the seventeenth century on the island of Barbados and are considered one of the "Seven Wonders of the Island of Barbados."

In 1823, Odet Philippe brought white grapefruits to Florida and planted them widely. By 1910 they were being grown in the suitable climates of Texas and California. Since the white grapefruits were so bitter for most palates, the sweeter red and pink varieties began to outsell them; by 1962 Florida had stopped growing white grapefruits altogether.

THE MANY USES OF WHITE GRAPEFRUITS

The bitter taste of white grapefruits works best in savory dishes such as salsas and ceviche.

WHERE THEY GROW

Today, white grapefruits are cultivated in California, Texas, Arizona, Morocco, Spain, Turkey, India, Israel, and South America.

AVAILABILITY

White grapefruits are available year-round, though they're best enjoyed from winter through spring.

Pomelo (Shaddock)

(Citrus maxima)

HISTORICAL BACKGROUND

The pomelo is a sweeter, firmer, and less juicy relative of the grapefruit. In fact, many presume the grapefruit originated from crossing a pomelo and an orange.

It is sometimes called a shaddock—a name that honors Philip Shaddock, the sea captain who first introduced pomelo seeds to the West Indies in the 1640s.

ATTRIBUTES

The pomelo is the largest of all citrus fruits. They can weigh up to 4 lb [1.8 kg], and wild fruits commonly weigh over 25 lb [11.3 kg]. The skin ranges from yellow to pink and is thicker than grapefruit skin. The flesh, which is divided into 11 to 18 segments separated by tough, inedible membranes, has a much milder taste than that of its grapefruit cousins.

THE MANY USES OF POMELO GRAPEFRUITS

Pomelos are consumed on many festive occasions across Asia. They are perfect for seafood, vegetable, and fruit salads.

WHERE THEY GROW

Today, pomelos are cultivated in California and Florida, across Asia, and in parts of Central and South America.

AVAILABILITY

Pomelos are available from early fall to late spring.

Melogold and Oroblanco Grapefruits

(Citrus paradisi Macfadyen)

HISTORICAL BACKGROUND

Melogold and oroblanco are grapefruits patented in 1981 and 1986, respectively, by Dr. Robert Soost and Dr. James Cameron at the University of California, Riverside. Both have been widely distributed into production by California growers. In 2000, they both patented the Pixie (page 122) and Gold Nugget mandarins.

ATTRIBUTES

Melogold and oroblanco grapefruits are from 4½ to 6 in [11 to 15 cm] in diameter, with a smooth, slightly textured skin. The Melogold is somewhat larger than the oroblanco, with slightly sweeter, milder flesh.

THE MANY USES OF MELOGOLD AND ORO-BLANCO GRAPEFRUITS

These grapefruits are best used for fresh applications, as the fruits' structure does not hold up through cooking or baking. They can be used in salads, as a topping for ice cream in a compote, or as a chutney for fish.

WHERE THEY GROW

Today, Melogold and oroblanco grapefruits are cultivated only in Southern California, where they were first patented.

AVAILABILITY

Both Melogold and oroblanco grapefruits are available from winter to spring.

Pink Grapefruit and Tomato Salsa

This tangy and slightly sweeter twist on a classic tomato salsa is a bright way to switch up your taco nights. The sweet-tart grapefruit pairs perfectly with juicy tomatoes, making it an ideal topping for grilled fish or chicken, or a fresh and flavorful dip for chips.

1 MEDIUM ONION, FINELY CHOPPED

1 LB [455 G] ROMA TOMATOES, FINELY CHOPPED

2 SERRANO CHILES, SEEDED AND FINELY CHOPPED

¼ CUP [10 G] FINELY CHOPPED CILANTRO

¼ CUP [96 G] FINELY CHOPPED PINK GRAPEFRUIT SEGMENTS

2 TBSP FRESHLY SQUEEZED GRAPEFRUIT JUICE

2 TSP GRANULATED SUGAR

2 TSP SALT

1. Rinse the chopped onion in a strainer under warm water for a few minutes. Shake dry.

2. Place the onion, tomatoes, chiles, cilantro, grapefruit, juice, sugar, and salt in a large bowl and toss to combine. The salsa will keep, refrigerated, for up to 3 days.

MAKES 4 CUPS [945 ML]

Shrimp, Grapefruit, and Avocado Salad

Light and refreshing but still packed with protein, this salad combines succulent shrimp, tangy grapefruit, and creamy avocado for a delightful, healthy meal. It's perfect for a summer lunch or a light dinner.

1 LB [455 G] (31 TO 40) SHRIMP, COOKED AND SHELLED

2 LARGE RED GRAPEFRUIT, SECTIONED

2 MEDIUM RIPE HASS AVOCADOS, SLICED

3 TBSP EXTRA-VIRGIN OLIVE OIL

2 TBSP FRESHLY SQUEEZED LEMON JUICE

1 TSP YELLOW MUSTARD

SALT

FRESHLY GROUND BLACK PEPPER

1. On a large platter, arrange the shrimp, grapefruit, and avocado in rows. Set aside.

2. In a jar with a tight-fitting lid, add the oil, lemon juice, mustard, salt, and pepper. Shake until the dressing is emulsified and thickened, about 20 seconds.

3. Drizzle the dressing over the shrimp, grapefruit, and avocado.

MAKES 4 SERVINGS

The Brown Derby's Grapefruit Cake

The iconic Brown Derby restaurant was open from 1926 to 1980 on Wilshire Boulevard, in Los Angeles, California. This renowned cake first appeared on the menu in 1936 when chef Harry Baker developed it for Louella Parsons, Hollywood's famous (or infamous, depending on whether you were the victim of one of her merciless exposés) gossip columnist, who requested a lower-calorie cake option with a bright-yet-creamy grapefruit frosting.

MAKES ONE
9 IN
[23CM]
ROUND CAKE
(ABOUT 12 SERVINGS)

CAKE

3 CUPS [360 G] CAKE FLOUR

1½ CUPS [300 G] GRANULATED SUGAR

1 TBSP BAKING POWDER

1½ TSP SEA SALT

CONT'D

1. To make the cake: Preheat the oven to 350°F [180°C]. Spray two 9 in [23 cm] round cake pans with nonstick spray.

2. In a large bowl, sift together the flour, sugar, baking powder, and salt. Make a well in the center and add the water, oil, egg yolks, grapefruit juice, and lemon zest. Mix until very smooth. Set aside.

cont'd

CAKE (cont'd)

½ CUP [120 ML] COLD WATER

½ CUP [120 ML] CANOLA OIL

6 EGGS, SEPARATED

6 TBSP [90 ML] FRESHLY SQUEEZED
GRAPEFRUIT JUICE

1 TSP LEMON ZEST

½ TSP CREAM OF TARTAR

GRAPEFRUIT CREAM CHEESE ICING

8 OZ [230 G] CREAM CHEESE, AT ROOM
TEMPERATURE

1 TBSP FRESHLY SQUEEZED GRAPEFRUIT
JUICE

2 TSP LEMON ZEST

4 CUPS [480 G] CONFECTIONERS'
SUGAR

1 LARGE GRAPEFRUIT, SECTIONED

3. In the bowl of a stand mixer fitted with the whip attachment, combine the egg whites and cream of tartar on low speed. Steadily increase the speed to high, and whip until the mixture begins to look thick and frothy, about 3 minutes. Continue whipping until the egg whites hold stiff peaks but do not look dry.

4. With a rubber spatula, carefully fold the flour mixture into the beaten egg whites until just combined.

5. Divide the batter between the two prepared cake pans. Bake until the top of the cake is golden brown and springs back when the center is pressed, about 30 minutes. Cool completely on baking racks.

6. While the cake cools, make the icing: In the bowl of a stand mixer fitted with the paddle attachment, blend the cream cheese, juice, zest, and confectioners' sugar on medium speed until smooth. Add three grapefruit sections to the icing, one at a time, mixing thoroughly after each addition.

7. To assemble the cake, place one layer on a cake plate or stand. Spread a layer of about ¼ cup [127 g] of icing on top and level out with a spatula. Repeat with the remaining layer. Ice the sides with the remaining icing.

8. Once assembled, decorate the top of the cake with the remaining grapefruit sections.

Grapefruit Mimosa Bonbons

Bright, bubbly, and deliciously tangy, these bonbons are the perfect bite-size treat for any celebration, but they're especially beloved for a New Year's Eve party.

¾ CUP [170 G] UNSALTED BUTTER, AT ROOM TEMPERATURE

7 CUPS [840 G] CONFECTIONERS' SUGAR, PLUS MORE AS NEEDED

2 TBSP GRAPEFRUIT ZEST

⅓ CUP [80 ML] BUBBLY WINE OF CHOICE (SEE NOTE)

¼ CUP [60 ML] FRESHLY SQUEEZED GRAPEFRUIT JUICE, PLUS MORE AS NEEDED

CONT'D

1. In the bowl of a stand mixer fitted with the paddle attachment, add the butter, confectioners' sugar, grapefruit zest, bubbly wine, and grapefruit juice. Turn the mixer to low speed and mix until just combined, then raise the speed to medium and beat for 2 minutes, until the mixture resembles a thick, creamy icing. If the mixture is too soft, add more confectioners' sugar; if too thick, add more grapefruit juice. Refrigerate the mixture for 15 minutes.

cont'd

MAKES 48 BONBONS

1 LB [455 G] WHITE CHOCOLATE, MELTED AND COOLED BUT KEPT LIQUID (SEE NOTE)

1 CUP [120 G] FINELY CHOPPED PECANS

2. Pour the melted white chocolate into a shallow dish, place the chopped pecans in a small bowl, and line a baking sheet with parchment paper. Scoop the chilled mixture into balls using a #100 cookie scoop. Add each ball to the white chocolate and gently roll to coat. Roll the coated ball in the nuts, turning to coat and gently pressing down into the nuts. Place on the prepared baking sheet and let stand at room temperature until hardened.

NOTE   **Keep the chocolate melted for dipping by setting the bowl over warm water; do not microwave.**

KUMQUAT

(CITRUS FORTUNELLA)

Tips on Use

Since the fruit is so tiny and the peel is entirely edible, zesting and juicing the kumquat is impossible, nor would you want to waste that gold! To best enjoy this citrus fruit, just give it a wash and eat it straight.

Kumquats, also known as mandarinquats, may be the smallest citrus fruit, but they majorly deliver on flavor. They are the only citrus that let you pop the entire fruit into your mouth like a grape, skin and all, and eat whole. If you've never tried one, get ready for a powerful little flavor bomb that packs a big punch.

NUTRITIONAL AND HEALTH BENEFITS OF KUMQUATS

The Cantonese word *kumquat* ("golden orange") was assigned to the fruit for the powerful health benefits it shares with oranges.

Kumquats are an excellent source of:

Vitamin C	Vitamin A
Dietary fiber	Calcium
Manganese	Vitamin E
Copper	
Trace amounts of iron, zinc, and potassium	

In traditional Chinese medicine, kumquats are used to remedy sore throats, congestion, and coughs. The fruits are traditionally mashed and mixed with ginger, salt, and honey, then steeped as a soothing tea, or chewed and swallowed raw.

Fukushu Kumquat

(Fortunella obovata 'Fukushu')

HISTORICAL BACKGROUND

Fukushu kumquats are native to Asia, where they've been growing wild since ancient times. Fukushu kumquats are believed to be a hybrid between two unknown kumquats. In 1864, the English citrus collector Robert Fortune introduced kumquats to North America and Europe.

ATTRIBUTES

The Fukushu is the largest of all the kumquats, averaging 1 to 3 in [2.5 to 7.5 cm] in length. The skin is golden yellow to dark orange, glossy and thin with a textured surface. The flesh is dense and thick, with six to eight segments and a few large cream-colored seeds. The entire fruit is edible (yes, even the seeds). The fruit is tangy, sweet, and sharp, with a floral flavor.

THE MANY USES OF FUKUSHU KUMQUATS

Fukushu kumquats are perfect for slicing into coins and tossing into a salad, chopping up into salsa, or pickling to create a garnish for drinks.

WHERE THEY GROW

Today, Fukushu kumquats are cultivated in Japan, Southern California, China, Chile, and parts of Southeast Asia.

AVAILABILITY

Fukushu kumquats are available year-round.

Nagami (Naga) Kumquat

(*Fortunella margarita*)

HISTORICAL BACKGROUND

In 1930, Dr. Walter Swingle, in partnership with the US Department of Agriculture, produced a kumquat citrus hybrid, the Nagami, among other citrus fruits. In 1930s China, the Nagami was used more often ornamentally as a dwarf tree, while America used it for its fruit.

ATTRIBUTES

The Nagami kumquat is olive-shaped, 1 to 2 in [2.5 to 5 cm] long. The skin is light orange.

THE MANY USES OF NAGAMI KUMQUATS

In its early days of cultivation, the Nagami was used only as an ornamental tree. Later the fruit was commonly made into a marmalade. Today, it is used for candies and sliced thinly for drinks and decorating.

WHERE THEY GROW

Today, Nagami kumquats are cultivated in Florida, California, and parts of Asia.

AVAILABILITY

Nagami kumquats are available in 1 lb [455 g] packages from fall through spring.

Chinese Kumquat

(Fortunella obovata 'Fukushu')

This kumquat variety is also known as fortunella and, in the early 1900s, as plum orange.

HISTORICAL BACKGROUND

In many Asian cultures, kumquats are a traditional symbol of the Lunar New Year as they represent prosperity, wealth, and good health.

In the early 1900s, Chinese kumquats were introduced to the United States as a seasonal holiday fruit in East Coast grocery advertisement campaigns. Both fresh and candied, Chinese kumquats were sold from growers in Florida.

ATTRIBUTES

Chinese kumquats are the smallest kumquat (and thus the very smallest citrus fruit), measuring a mere ½ in [13 mm]. They are light orange with a sweet peel and a tart interior.

THE MANY USES OF CHINESE KUMQUATS

Chinese kumquats are commonly candied, dipped in chocolate, or made into preserves.

WHERE THEY GROW

Today, Chinese kumquats are cultivated in Florida, California, Japan, and in English hothouses.

AVAILABILITY

Chinese kumquats are available from late fall to early winter.

Kumquat and Chile Baked Salmon

SERVES 4

Here's a hearty, healthy dinner for busy weeknights when you need to get food on the table, and fast. Umami baked salmon paired with a tangy kumquat glaze with a hint of chile is the perfect way to use up any kumquats you have sitting in the fruit basket.

4 OZ [115 G] KUMQUATS, SLICED THIN

2 JALAPENO PEPPERS, SEEDED AND CHOPPED

2 TBSP GRANULATED SUGAR

ZEST AND JUICE OF 1 MEDIUM LEMON

1 TBSP WHITE WINE VINEGAR

FOUR 6 OZ [170 G] SALMON FILLETS

1 TBSP CANOLA OIL

SALT

FRESHLY GROUND BLACK PEPPER

1. In a small saucepan on medium-high heat, combine the kumquats, jalapenos, sugar, zest, and vinegar with 1 cup of water. Cook, stirring occasionally, until the liquid has thickened, 14 to 16 minutes.

2. Remove from the heat, stir in the lemon juice, and set aside.

3. Pat the salmon with a paper towel to blot off any moisture. Heat the oil in a large sauté pan on medium heat. Add the salmon, skin-side down, and season with salt and pepper. Cook for 8 minutes, browning and crisping the skin before moving or flipping the fillets.

4. Turn over the fillets and sear for 1 minute more. Transfer to a serving plate and top with the kumquat sauce.

Kumquat and Pineapple Chutney

This is an ideal condiment for grilled meats, a spread for sandwiches, or a unique spread for your next charcuterie board. It adds a burst of tropical brightness to any dish, especially in the dead of winter, when you need it most!

1 CUP [200 G] GRANULATED SUGAR

½ CUP [120 ML] WHITE VINEGAR

1 LB [455 G] KUMQUATS, HALVED

8 OZ [230 G] CRUSHED PINEAPPLE, FRESH OR CANNED AND DRAINED

1 MEDIUM ONION, CHOPPED

½ CUP [70 G] GOLDEN RAISINS

¼ CUP [60 ML] FRESHLY SQUEEZED LIME JUICE

2 TBSP LIME ZEST

1 GARLIC CLOVE, MINCED

1 TSP MUSTARD SEEDS

¼ TSP CAYENNE PEPPER

1. In a stock pot on medium heat, bring the sugar and vinegar to a boil. Add the kumquats, pineapple, onion, raisins, lime juice and zest, garlic, mustard seeds, and cayenne. Simmer, uncovered, stirring occasionally, until thickened, 30 to 45 minutes.

2. Let cool and place in a covered container. The chutney will keep, refrigerated, for up to a week.

Makes about
3 CUPS
[720 ml]

Chinese Kumquat Chicken with Roasted Vegetables

Makes **4** *servings*

The sweet-tart pop of flavor from Chinese kumquats beautifully complements this savory chicken dish.

2 TBSP OLIVE OIL

1 PINT [450 G] KUMQUATS, HALVED (RESERVE 10 HALVES FOR GARNISH)

1 BROWN ONION, QUARTERED

¼ CUP [85 G] HONEY

SALT

FRESHLY GROUND BLACK PEPPER

12 SPRIGS FRESH THYME

ONE 3 LB [1.4 KG] CHICKEN, CUT INTO QUARTERS

1 TBSP DRIED MARJORAM

4 LARGE CARROTS (ABOUT 10½ OZ [300 G]), SLICED

CONT'D

1. Preheat the oven to 375°F [190°C] and set the racks to accommodate both a baking dish and a large roasting pan.

2. In a 9 by 13 in [23 by 33 cm] baking dish, combine the oil, kumquats, onion, and honey, making sure that the kumquats are thoroughly coated with the oil and honey. Season with salt and pepper. Scatter with half of the thyme sprigs.

3. Place the chicken on top of the kumquat/onion mixture. Spoon the oil and honey over each chicken piece to coat. Season well with salt and pepper. Strip the leaves from the remaining thyme sprigs and arrange the leaves on top of the chicken. Sprinkle with the marjoram.

cont'd

2 MEDIUM ZUCCHINIS (ABOUT 12¾ OZ [360 G]), SLICED

6 MEDIUM RED POTATOES (ABOUT 2¼ LB [1 KG]), CUT INTO PIECES

1 HEAD GARLIC, CLOVES PEELED

OLIVE OIL

1 TBSP FRESH THYME LEAVES

4. Cover the dish with foil and bake for one hour, then uncover and bake until well browned, about 30 minutes more.

5. While the chicken is cooking, prepare the carrots, zucchini, and potatoes in a large roasting pan. Coat well with olive oil, sprinkle with the thyme, and season with salt and pepper. Cover with foil and bake until fork tender, about 40 minutes.

6. Serve the chicken and vegetables together, garnished with the reserved kumquats.

LEM ON

(CITRUS LIMON)

Lemons are found in every cook's kitchen because of their versatility, flavor, and accessibility. They are among the world's most beloved dessert flavors, ranking beside vanilla and chocolate. But lemon isn't just for sweets; its exhilarating zing brings out the flavors of savory dishes, too.

Lemon trees are easy to grow in an amenable climate, and within a year will yield fruit season after season.

NUTRITIONAL AND HEALTH BENEFITS OF LEMONS

Lemons are more than just a folk remedy for colds and other respiratory ailments; the science backs this up. They are a good source of:

Vitamin C

Potassium

Calcium

Magnesium

Tips on Use

In addition to rolling the lemon on the counter as with other citrus, you can also microwave it for 10 to 15 seconds to soften the fruit and inner membranes to release the juice. Meyer lemons are thin-skinned, so microwaving is unnecessary.

Eureka Lemon

(*Citrus limon* 'Eureka')

HISTORICAL BACKGROUND

The Eureka lemon was bred in California in 1858 from selections made from seeds imported from Sicily.

One of the pioneers of the city of Riverside, California, was Luther Myrick Holt, an editor of the Riverside Daily Press. In Holt's time, most of the region's newspapers focused on citrus production before shifting to general news coverage.

In the mid-1880s, Holt created local citrus fairs for growers to highlight their new lemons and other citrus varieties. The San Gabriel Valley Citrus Fair and the Riverside Citrus Fair were among the first to mount a Eureka lemon display, to great success and fanfare.

In 1886, Holt took his citrus fairs on the road with the Southern California Fruit Growers' Association and organized the Southern California Citrus Fair in Chicago. The Midwest consumers were thrilled with the Eureka lemon's ability to travel cross-country by train and still be tree-fresh; it was a testament to that sunny Californian agricultural magic that's become an essential element of the West Coast's reputation.

ATTRIBUTES

Eureka lemons are the most widely grown lemon; these are the familiar lemons you find at the supermarket. Oblong and slightly egg-shaped, they average 3 to 3½ in [7.5 to 9 cm] in diameter. The peel is moderately thin, with a skin ranging from pale to bright yellow; a bitter white pith is hidden underneath. The zest contains aromatic oils. The zest and juice are highly acidic, creating a tangy flavor profile with understated sweetness.

THE MANY USES OF EUREKA LEMONS

From summer lemonade to salads, savory cooking to baked treats, Eureka lemons are the choice of home cooks and professionals worldwide. Known for its high juice content, the Eureka lemon is perfect for recipes that call for freshly squeezed lemon juice. Its texture also makes it easier to zest.

WHERE THEY GROW

Today, Eurekas are the most widely grown lemon, cultivated in Southern California, South Africa, Israel, Australia, and Argentina.

AVAILABILITY

Eurekas are winter-producing lemons, but in coastal growing areas they also produce two or three small crops in spring and summer, thus creating a year-round crop.

Lisbon Lemon

(Citrus limon 'Lisbon')

HISTORICAL BACKGROUND

In the early nineteenth century, the Lisbon lemon was named after the capital of Portugal, an homage to its country of origin with its favorable growing conditions.

Lisbon lemon trees made their international debut in the early 1800s, when they were imported to Australia, chosen for its similar temperatures and other growing conditions.

In 1875, the steamer *Mikado* crossed the Pacific Ocean from Australia to San Francisco, bringing the first Lisbon lemon trees to California. Thomas Andrew Garey, a horticulturist and the owner of the Childs' Nursery in downtown Los Angeles, grafted and grew thousands of Lisbon lemon trees for production. In 1878 alone, Garey sold over seventy-five thousand trees—fourteen thousand of them to Lucky Baldwin of Santa Anita Rancho in California. Three years later, lemon producer and California State Assembly member (a true Renaissance man!) Elmer Wallace Holmes of Riverside purchased trees from Garey. He marketed his lemons by wrapping each in paper emblazoned with "Lisbon Lemons from Riverside, California."

ATTRIBUTES

Lisbon lemons average 3 to 3½ in [7.5 to 9 cm] in diameter and have smooth, bright yellow skin. They have a tart flavor and an extremely high juice content. Some culinary professionals feel the Lisbon lemon has a slightly more acidic taste than Eureka lemons and use them for pastry and dressings.

THE MANY USES OF LISBON LEMONS

Although most lemon varieties are inter-changeable in recipes and other uses, the Lisbon lemon seems more acidic. When using them in desserts and other sweets, you may want to boost the sweetening in your recipe.

WHERE THEY GROW

Today, Lisbon lemons are cultivated in climates similar to that of their native Portugal: Spain, Sicily, and the Calabria regions of Italy; the San Diego and Riverside areas of California; New South Wales and Victoria in Australia; and the Western Cape of South Africa.

AVAILABILITY

Lisbon lemons are available year-round.

Seedless Lemon

(*Citrus limon* (L.) Osbeck)

HISTORICAL BACKGROUND

In 1939, Lasscock's Nursery in South Australia, the premier seedless lemon nursery, sent a cutting to the University of California, Riverside. The flavor is similar to the Lisbon but slightly less bitter. This import launched the growing and cultivating of seedless lemons in the United States.

ATTRIBUTES

Seedless lemons are around 3 in [7.5 cm] in diameter. The skin is similar to that of the Lisbon lemon—smooth and bright yellow. As with many "seedless" fruits, the moniker is a bit exaggerated; on average, there's one seed in each lemon.

THE MANY USES OF SEEDLESS LEMONS

Initially seedless lemons were available only to the food trade; restaurants used them to reduce time and waste. They can be used like any other lemon, and the best part: You won't have to fish out those slippery, elusive seeds.

WHERE THEY GROW

Today, seedless lemons are cultivated in Australia and Southern California.

AVAILABILITY

Seedless lemons are available from November to May.

Variegated Pink Eureka Lemon

(*Citrus limon* 'Variegated Pink'), also known as a zebra lemon or pink lemonade lemon

HISTORICAL BACKGROUND

A mutation was discovered on an ordinary Eureka lemon tree in the backyard of a home in Burbank, California, and was then researched. Today, these pink beauties are a celebrated member of the lemon family, praised for their beautiful and distinctive hue.

ATTRIBUTES

Variegated Pink Eureka lemons are 2 to 2½ in [5 to 6 cm] in diameter. The skin is at first striped green over a yellow base, giving them the moniker "zebra lemon." As the fruit ripens, the stripes begin to fade. The flesh is light pink and the juice a lighter, yellowish pink, almost colorless. This lemon has few seeds and a very acidic flavor profile.

THE MANY USES OF PINK VARIEGATED LEMONS

Pink lemons pair nicely with lavender, rosemary, marjoram, and thyme. They make for a wonderful drink garnish.

WHERE THEY GROW

Today, pink lemons are cultivated in Southern California, Arizona, Texas, and Florida.

AVAILABILITY

Pink lemons are harvested mainly in the summer but are available year-round in coastal areas.

Meyer Lemon

(Citrus meyeri)

HISTORICAL BACKGROUND

A hybrid citrus, this renowned lemon is native to Beijing, China. It is believed to be a cross between a lemon and a mandarin, or possibly some other sweet orange, like a tangerine.

On June 11, 1908, Frank N. Meyer, a US Department of Agriculture plant explorer, returned to San Francisco after a three-year exploration in China and other parts of Asia on the Standard Oil steamer *Ashtabula*. Meyer had collected bamboo, soybeans, spruces, and two white-cheeked gibbon monkeys captured in the mountains north of Peking for the zoological gardens in Washington. But his chief cargo was fifteen tons of young trees—among them a dwarf lemon tree that produced what we now know as Meyer lemons.

When Frank Meyer came back from his voyages, he landed in Chico, California, making Chico the first US location to grow Meyer lemon trees. These were grown mainly as a backyard crop, not for mass production.

In the 1980s, home-and-hospitality doyenne Martha Stewart and restaurateur Alice Waters, owner of the famous and beloved Chez Panisse, elevated the Meyer lemon to star status with the help of the media.

ATTRIBUTES

There's a strong visual distinction between Meyer lemons and any other lemons. Meyers are rounded ovals from 2½ to 3 inches [6 to 7.5 cm] in diameter. The outer skin is classic lemon yellow with a touch of orange.

Because of the Meyer's thin, fragrant, oily peel, the fruit has never been commercially available, as shipping the fruit would damage the skin. The flesh and juice are lower in acid, sweeter, and more aromatic than other lemon varieties, with a distinctive floral character.

THE MANY USES OF MEYER LEMONS

The juice of the Meyer can be used in place of any other common lemon juice, with the understanding that it's sweeter and less acidic. Lemon curd and other pastries made with the Meyer are exceptionally flavorful.

WHERE THEY GROW

Today, the Meyer is sold mainly at local farmers' markets in Southern California, Florida, and Texas.

AVAILABILITY

Meyer lemons are mainly available during the fall and winter months.

Chicken Piccata

A sunny Italian classic that harnesses the bright power of the lemon, Chicken Piccata offers a master class in the art of balancing citrus with richness.

SERVES 4

FOUR 6 OZ [170 G] BONELESS, SKINLESS CHICKEN BREASTS

⅓ CUP [45 G] ALL-PURPOSE FLOUR

½ TSP SALT

½ TSP FRESHLY GROUND BLACK PEPPER

2 TBSP GRATED PARMESAN CHEESE

4 TBSP [60 ML] EXTRA-VIRGIN OLIVE OIL

4 TBSP [55 G] UNSALTED BUTTER, AT ROOM TEMPERATURE

½ CUP [120 ML] CHICKEN STOCK OR DRY WHITE WINE

¼ CUP [60 ML] FRESHLY SQUEEZED LEMON JUICE

¼ CUP [45 G] CAPERS

FRESH LEMON SLICES, FOR GARNISH (OPTIONAL)

¼ CUP [10 G] FRESHLY CHOPPED PARSLEY

1. Set a roasting pan on a rack in the oven.

2. If the chicken pieces are thick, place them between two pieces of plastic wrap and pound them with a meat tenderizer to ¼ in [6 mm] thickness. Pat dry with a paper towel and set aside.

3. Preheat the oven to 350°F [180°C]. In a small bowl, mix the flour, salt, pepper, and grated Parmesan. Place on a shallow plate. Dredge the chicken in the mixture until well coated.

4. In a large skillet on medium heat, heat half of the olive oil and butter. Add two of the chicken breasts; do not crowd the pan. Cook until well browned on each side, about 3 minutes per side. Transfer the chicken to the pan in the oven. Cook the other two breasts in the same manner and add to the pan. Reserve the skillet with its drippings.

cont'd

5. Bake until the chicken reads 145°F [63°C] on an instant-read thermometer, 20 to 24 minutes.

6. While the chicken is baking, add the chicken stock, lemon juice, and capers to the skillet with its drippings. Cook on medium heat, using a spatula to scrape up the browned bits and stirring occasionally until the sauce is reduced by half, about 5 minutes. Whisk in the remaining butter and olive oil. Place the chicken on a serving plate and pour the sauce over it. Place the lemon slices (if using) on top of the chicken. Sprinkle with the parsley and serve.

Tangy Lemon Mist Cookies

These light, crunchy, lemony cookies make a wonderful crust for cheesecakes. Drench the cookies with powdered sugar or dip them partially in melted chocolate for a finished look. If you've got Tart Lemon Curd (page 67) on hand, you can also sandwich some between two cookies.

3 CUPS [420 G] ALL-PURPOSE FLOUR

⅛ TSP SALT

1 TSP BAKING SODA

1 TSP CREAM OF TARTAR

½ CUP [113 G] UNSALTED BUTTER, AT ROOM TEMPERATURE

1½ CUPS [300 G] GRANULATED SUGAR

1 LARGE EGG

CONT'D

1. In a large bowl, combine the flour, salt, baking soda, and cream of tartar. Set aside.

2. In the bowl of a stand mixer fitted with the paddle attachment, blend the butter, 1 cup [200 g] of the sugar, and the egg, oil, juice, vanilla, lemon extract, and zest on medium speed. Mix until well combined.

3. Add the flour mixture to the butter mixture. Blend until fully incorporated.

4. Chill for 30 minutes for best results.

cont'd

MAKES 3 DOZEN

½ CUP [120 ML] CANOLA OIL

3 TBSP FRESHLY SQUEEZED LEMON JUICE

½ TSP VANILLA EXTRACT

⅓ TSP LEMON EXTRACT OR TWO DROPS OF LEMON OIL

2 TSP LEMON ZEST

5. Preheat the oven to 350°F [180°C] and line two baking sheets with parchment paper. Working with pieces of dough about the size of a large walnut, roll them between your palms into a ball. Roll each ball in the remaining ½ cup [100 g] of granulated sugar and set 2 in [5 cm] apart on the prepared pans.

6. Bake until light brown, 10 to 12 minutes. Cool on a rack. They will keep in a covered container for up to a week.

Tart Lemon Curd

With just four ingredients, this velvety lemon curd is a hardworking, versatile recipe that works beautifully in cakes and pastries, spread on a piece of toast, or (if you're anything like me) eaten with a spoon, straight from the bowl. For a very tart curd, as for the filling on a cake, use Lisbon lemons; for a sweeter dessert, use Meyer.

10 LARGE EGG YOLKS

¾ CUP [150 G] GRANULATED SUGAR

¾ CUP [180 ML] LEMON JUICE (MEYER OR LISBON)

½ CUP [113 G] UNSALTED BUTTER, CUBED, AT ROOM TEMPERATURE

1 PINT [480 g]

1. In the bottom of a double boiler, heat water to a simmer.

2. In the top bowl of the double boiler, off the heat, whisk the egg yolks to break them up; while whisking, sprinkle in the sugar. Still whisking, pour in the lemon juice in a steady stream.

3. Set the bowl over the simmering water. Do not allow the water to boil. Cook, stirring constantly, until the mixture coats the back of a large spoon, about 7 minutes.

4. Remove from the heat. Whisk in the pieces of butter, a few at a time, until melted and smooth.

5. Cool and allow to set before using.

6. To store, after the curd reaches room temperature, transfer to an airtight container. It will keep, refrigerated, for up to a week.

World's Best Lemonade

Makes about
2 QUARTS [1.9 L]

There's not much to it: tart lemons, fine sugar, warm water. Mix them together and you get sunshine in a glass. If you like, you can use pink lemons and the drink will be light pink.

2 CUPS [400 G] SUPERFINE OR BAKER'S SUGAR

1 CUP [240 ML] WARM WATER

4 CUPS [960 ML] COLD WATER

2 CUPS [480 ML] FRESHLY SQUEEZED LEMON JUICE

ICE CUBES

2 MEDIUM LEMONS, CUT INTO THIN SLICES

1. In a small saucepan on medium heat, bring the sugar and warm water to a low boil. Set aside and let cool completely.

2. Pour the cooled sugar syrup into a large pitcher. Add the cold water and lemon juice and blend.

3. To serve, place ice cubes in a tall glass and fill with lemonade. Garnish with lemon slices.

VARIATIONS:

- To make a fizzy drink, use lemon tonic water in place of the cold water.

- For an adult version, add 1½ oz [45 ml] of lemon vodka or Limoncello.

LIME

(CITRUS AURANTIFOLIA)

Tips on Use

In addition to rolling the lime on the counter as with other citrus, you can also microwave it for 10 to 15 seconds to soften the fruit and inner membranes to release the juice.

Limes are the universally beloved small, round green fruits that have only recently been given the credit they deserve. Limes add zesty flavor to ordinary meals, transforming an otherwise ordinary dish into an extraordinary delight. Their vibrant green color and tangy taste make every sip of a cocktail or garnished glass of water instantly transport you to a tropical island vacation.

NUTRITIONAL AND HEALTH BENEFITS OF LIMES

Like their cousin the lemon, limes offer a treasure trove of health benefits. A few tablespoons of lime juice in a glass of water can be drunk to ease stomach pain and hydrate. Lime essential oil packs an immune-boosting punch, but use it only after sun exposure, not before.

Limes are a good source of:

Vitamin C

Antioxidants

Flavonoids & limonoids

Potassium

Calcium

Magnesium

Persian Lime

(Citrus latifolia)

This variety is also known as Tahitian lime or Bearss lime (a seedless variety).

HISTORICAL BACKGROUND

It is believed that Persian limes originated in Tahiti as a hybrid fruit, a cross between lemon and Key lime. They got their name as they were brought by fruit traders from Asia to the Middle East.

Persian limes were first introduced to the United States in the nineteenth century. They have become the predominant commercial lime, a testament to their popularity and versatility.

The seedless Bearss lime was first cultivated in the late 1800s by John Theodore Bearss at W. H. Grant Place orchards in Porterville, California.

Persian limes flourish in tropical and subtropical climates in full sunlight. They need consistent watering, whether by rainfall or irrigation, until the soil is moist but not soaked. To ensure consistent quality, Persian limes are propagated through grafting rather than seeds. They're also harvested by hand rather than by machine, to prevent bruises and other damage to the fruit. These are the most popular variety of limes that you'll find at your local grocery store.

ATTRIBUTES

The Persian lime fruit is the largest of all limes, 2 to 2½ in [5 to 6 cm] in diameter, about the size of a ping-pong ball. The skin is a shiny dark, bright green, turning yellow when fully ripe in the fall months. They're known for their subtly tart and mild flavor.

THE MANY USES OF PERSIAN LIMES

The juice of a Persian lime is versatile; it can be used anywhere you'd want a fresh, floral-forward citrus flavor, such as a marinade for fish, salad dressings, and beverages.

The zest and juice can be used in sweet and savory dishes from pasta to cookies, and in drinks such as margaritas, mojitos, gin and tonics, and the Moscow Mule (page 91), concocted in 1941 and made famous in a 1948 New York Herald Tribune article. Limes, in both their fresh and preserved form, are used widely in Latin American, Southeast Asian, and Middle Eastern cuisines in dishes such as ceviche, Thai curries, and Persian stews.

WHERE THEY GROW

Today, Mexico, Florida, and California are the central regions where Persian limes are grown.

AVAILABILITY

Persian limes are available year-round in most markets. The prime growing season is from August to February.

Key Lime

(Citrus aurantifolia)

Key limes are also known as Mexican limes, bartender limes, or West Indian limes.

HISTORICAL BACKGROUND

Key limes are believed to have originated in Southeast Asia. They were first brought to the Florida Keys by Spanish explorers in the 1500s; thus the little citrus fruit was named the Key lime. They were exclusively grown commercially in Southern Florida until a catastrophic hurricane destroyed the crop in the fall of 1926.

ATTRIBUTES

Key limes are smaller than other limes, from 1 to 1½ in [2.5 to 4 cm] in diameter. The skin is yellow when fully ripe, but most Key limes are sold while still green, packed in mesh bags. Key limes are often harvested for shipping when fully grown but still green, as they continue to ripen after being plucked from the tree. They are packed with seeds and have a strong floral aroma and a distinctive, tangy flavor that is more intense and slightly more acidic than that of Persian limes. This makes them particularly popular in cooking and baking, despite being more labor intensive to juice due to their petite size and high seed count.

THE MANY USES OF KEY LIMES
The most popular use is, of course, the classic Key lime pie, but the juice is also used in marinades, dressings, desserts, and cocktails. The zest of Key limes is also used to flavor baked goods and savory dishes.

WHERE THEY GROW
Today, Key limes are still grown in Southern Florida as well as parts of Central America and Mexico.

AVAILABILITY
Key limes are available in specialty stores and large cities year-round. The peak season is June through September. If you can't find Key limes in your area, you can use Persian limes; the result will be similar, though without the distinctive flavor and aroma.

Finger Lime

(*Microcitrus australasica*)

The finger lime is a unique lime variety, native to Australia. They are often called "caviar limes" for the fish-egg appearance of the flavorful beads (vesicles) extracted from the small fruit, the size and shape of a chubby finger. Finger limes have recently gained popularity among chefs and pastry chefs for their ability to transform a dessert or dish with their distinctive beauty and textural charm.

HISTORICAL BACKGROUND

The finger lime was discovered and used by Aboriginal communities in the rainforest areas of Australia. Finger limes were used in food, as an antiseptic for skin infections, and to heal wounds.

ATTRIBUTES

Sold in small baskets like cherry tomatoes, finger limes are small and elongated, 2 to 4 in [5 to 10 cm] long, roughly shaped like a finger—hence the name. The skin can range from dark green to black. The flesh, ranging from green to light pink, forms tiny, crisp, pearl-like "caviar" that pop in your mouth, releasing delicious tangy juice with an herbaceous body. Each finger lime will yield just 1 tsp [5 ml] of pearls, a testament to their rarity and value.

THE MANY USES OF FINGER LIMES

The caviar-like beads of a finger lime add flavor and a unique texture to seafood dishes, cocktails, salads, and desserts. The beads can be used in salsas, dressings, and sauces for an extra tangy kick. In drinks like sparkling water, cocktails, and mocktails they add visual appeal. They can also be sprinkled over cakes, tarts, and ice cream for a pretty and refreshing citrusy touch.

WHERE THEY GROW

Today, finger limes are mainly grown in Queensland and New South Wales, Australia, and the Central Coast of California.

AVAILABILITY

Finger limes are seasonally harvested from June through December.

Shrimp and Sea Bass Ceviche with Finger Limes

SERVES 4

Serve up this appetizer however you like: with a bowl of plantain chips, on top of some shredded lettuce as a salad, or in a tortilla for a ceviche taco. If you're in the mood for something heartier, try it atop a mound of pasta.

8 OZ [230 G] 70/90 BAY SHRIMP (RAW), SLICED INTO SMALL PIECES

8 OZ [230 G] SEA BASS, DEBONED AND CUT INTO SMALL PIECES

¾ CUP [180 ML] FRESHLY SQUEEZED PERSIAN LIME JUICE

2 MEDIUM ROMA TOMATOES, SEEDED AND DICED

1 SMALL RED ONION, DICED

⅓ CUP [15 G] FRESH CILANTRO, CHOPPED (LEAVES ONLY)

¼ CUP [15 G] FRESH OREGANO, CHOPPED (LEAVES ONLY)

4 FINGER LIMES, SLICED LENGTHWISE, EXPOSING THE "PEARLS"

1. Place the shrimp and sea bass in a shallow bowl. Pour the lime juice over them, cover with plastic wrap, and refrigerate for 2 to 4 hours, until no longer opaque. Drain and discard the lime juice and place in a medium bowl.

2. Add the tomatoes, onion, cilantro, and oregano and stir gently to distribute. Chill for at least 1 hour. When ready to serve, spoon the finger lime pearls on top. The ceviche will keep, refrigerated, for up to 2 days.

Ginger Lime Caramelized Scallops

4 Servings

Preparing scallops is a surefire way to impress guests, but the real secret is that they're an ultra easy dish to prepare, requiring just a touch of caution to avoid overcooking, which will turn them rubbery. The Key lime juice mixed with spicy ginger adds a lively zing to the buttery richness of the scallops.

¼ CUP [60 ML] KEY LIME JUICE

1 TBSP GRANULATED SUGAR

1 TBSP LOW-SODIUM SOY SAUCE

1 TSP PEELED AND MINCED FRESH GINGER

8 SEA SCALLOPS (ABOUT 12 OZ [340 G]), DRIED WELL WITH PAPER TOWELS

3 TBSP NEUTRAL OIL

1. In a medium bowl, whisk together the lime juice, sugar, soy sauce, and ginger with 2 Tbsp [30 ml] of water to combine.

2. Add the scallops, turning to coat. Cover the bowl with plastic wrap and let marinate in the refrigerator for 15 minutes.

cont'd

3. Heat the oil in a skillet on medium heat and warm a serving dish. Remove the scallops from the mixture, reserving the marinade, and add to the skillet, being careful to not overcrowd the pan; cook in two stages if necessary. Cook until lightly brown and firm when touched, 1 to 2 minutes on each side; do not overcook. Place the cooked scallops on the warmed dish.

4. In the same skillet, add the reserved marinade and cook on medium heat until thickened, about 5 minutes. Pour the sauce over the cooked scallops. Serve immediately while still hot.

Mojito Tea Cake with Rum Glaze

This loaf cake is bursting with the fresh Cuban flavors of its famous namesake cocktail, the Mojito. It can be made several days ahead and refrigerated, covered, until needed.

MAKES ONE **1 LB** [455 G] **CAKE** (ABOUT 12 SERVINGS)

1 TBSP + 2 TSP FRESH LIME ZEST (FROM ABOUT 3 PERSIAN LIMES)

¾ CUP + 1 TBSP [195 ML] FRESHLY SQUEEZED LIME JUICE (FROM ABOUT 8 PERSIAN LIMES)

CAKE

1 CUP [200 G] GRANULATED SUGAR

⅓ CUP [80 ML] CANOLA OIL

2 EGGS

1½ CUPS [180 G] CAKE FLOUR

1 TSP BAKING POWDER

¼ TSP BAKING SODA

½ TSP SALT

⅓ CUP [80 G] SOUR CREAM

CONT'D

TO MAKE THE CAKE

1. Preheat the oven to 350°F [180°C]. Spray a 1 lb [455 g] loaf pan (8½ by 4½ by 2½ in [21.5 by 11 by 6 cm]) with nonstick spray.

2. In a medium bowl, blend 1 Tbsp of the lime zest, the granulated sugar, and the oil. Whisk in the eggs until thoroughly blended. Set aside.

3. In another medium bowl, whisk together the flour, baking powder, baking soda, and salt. Add to the sugar-egg mixture and mix thoroughly.

cont'd

CAKE (cont'd)

¼ CUP [10 G] FRESH MINT LEAVES, CHOPPED FINE

FRESH LIME SLICES, FOR GARNISH (OPTIONAL)

ICING

1 CUP [120 G] CONFECTIONERS' SUGAR

GLAZE

1 TBSP GRANULATED SUGAR

2 TBSP CLEAR RUM

4. In a small bowl, combine ¼ cup [60 ml] of the lime juice and the sour cream, blending well. Stir into the batter and fold in the chopped mint. Pour into the prepared pan. Bake on the center rack for 45 to 55 minutes; a toothpick inserted into the center should come out clean.

5. Meanwhile, make the icing and glaze.

TO MAKE THE ICING

6. Whisk together the confectioners' sugar, 1 Tbsp of the lime juice, and the remaining 2 tsp of lime zest until smooth. Set aside.

TO MAKE THE GLAZE

7. In a small saucepan on low heat, stir together the granulated sugar and the remaining ½ cup [120 ml] of lime juice until dissolved. Remove from the heat and add the rum.

8. As soon as the cake comes out of the oven, while still in the pan, pour the glaze over it. Let it set for 10 minutes, then invert the cake from the pan onto a serving plate. Pour the icing over the top and garnish with lime slices (if using).

No-Bake Key Lime Pie

Makes
6
servings

Indulge in the tangy and refreshing flavor of a Key lime pie, a dessert reminiscent of those found in the pie shops on Duval Street in Key West. This recipe is a cinch, requiring just five ingredients and no baking time or oven heat, so it's perfect for entertaining on a warm and lazy summer day.

¾ CUP [180 ML] HEAVY CREAM

ONE 14 OZ [415 ML] CAN SWEETENED CONDENSED MILK

½ CUP [120 ML] FRESHLY SQUEEZED KEY LIME JUICE

2 TSP FRESH KEY LIME ZEST

ONE 9 IN [23 CM] STORE-BOUGHT GRAHAM CRACKER CRUST

1. In a medium bowl, using a hand mixer, whip the cream until soft peaks form, about 5 minutes.

2. In a separate large bowl, combine the sweetened condensed milk, lime juice, and half of the zest. Fold in 1 cup [240 ml] of the freshly whipped cream.

3. Pour the filling into the prepared crust. Transfer the remaining whipped cream to a pastry bag. Pipe 6 evenly spaced swirls of whipped cream onto the surface, one for each slice, then sprinkle the remaining zest on top.

4. Refrigerate for 2 hours or until firm. Slice and serve.

The Cock'n Bull's Moscow Mule

This drink was originally invented in the 1940s at the Cock'n Bull restaurant on Sunset Boulevard in West Hollywood. Although not a must, it's best served in a classic copper mug, which keeps the drink at a cool temperature.

1½ OZ [45 ML] VODKA

FRESHLY SQUEEZED JUICE OF ½ PERSIAN LIME

8 OZ [240 ML] GINGER BEER, PREFERABLY COCK'N BULL BRAND

1 LIME WEDGE

In a copper mug filled with ice, add the vodka and lime juice. Top with the ginger beer. Garnish with the lime wedge.

MAKES ONE DRINK

OR
AN
GE

(CITRUS SINENSIS)

Oranges are a cherished gift of bright, sunny cheer that reaches the peak of sweet juiciness in the dead of winter. The humble orange captures the light of summer and regifts it when we need it most. For this reason, whenever I see an orange tree around my neighborhood, I call it a "Happy Tree."

NUTRITIONAL AND HEALTH BENEFITS OF ORANGES

One orange provides the full daily dose of vitamin C. Every part of the orange—from peel to pulp—has a use, whether in cooking, baking, or juicing. Oranges are an excellent source of:

Vitamin C

Dietary fiber

Potassium

Calcium

Tips on Use

All parts of an orange are helpful in everyday life. The skin can help whiten teeth and reduce bad breath. The oils from the skin can be used to clean and polish wood furniture and eliminate odors.

Washington Navel Orange

(Citrus sinensis)

HISTORICAL BACKGROUND

The Washington navel orange is arguably the most essential and ubiquitous crop ever introduced in the United States. The Washington navel is named after the first president, not the state. This fruit's introduction in California started the state's second "Gold Rush," but instead of the precious metal, the gold in question was the sunny hue of the navel orange's skin.

In 1873, Eliza Maria Lovell Tibbets brought two navel orange trees to California for her new home in Riverside. The entire navel orange acreage in California is descended from those parent trees.

Tibbets had secured the trees from William Saunders of the Department of Agriculture while living in Washington, DC. The two trees proved to be exceptionally more bountiful than any other orange tree on the market. The fruits' size, appearance, texture, and seedlessness soon gained them a following. In 1878, the navel orange won first prize at the Southern California Horticultural Fair. And within four years, Southern California was home to over half a million navel orange trees.

In 1902, one of Tibbets's original trees was replanted on the corner of Arlington and Magnolia Streets, close to downtown Riverside. A year later, the second tree was acquired by Frank A. Miller, founder of the Glenwood Mission Inn; with the help of President Teddy Roosevelt it was replanted in the hotel's courtyard. In 1921, the tree died and was replaced by an eleven-year-old descendant. Today, you can see the stock of the original parent tree revivified with new roots and surrounded with protective fencing.

ATTRIBUTES

The navel orange is a medium-size fruit, 3 to 4 in [7.5 to 10 cm] in diameter, rounded and slightly oval. The trademark "navel" forms on the blossom end of the fruit. The skin is smooth, with a lightly pebbled texture. The flesh is a translucent yellow-orange, divided into 10 to 12 segments.

THE MANY USES OF WASHINGTON NAVEL ORANGES

Navels are the most popular oranges for baked and savory culinary uses, such as fruit segments for fresh salads, desserts, salsas, citrus marinades, and marmalades. Navels are the easiest to peel for a fresh seedless treat.

WHERE THEY GROW

Today, navel oranges are cultivated worldwide in Brazil, Southern California, Paraguay, South Africa, Australia, Japan, and Spain.

AVAILABILITY

Washington navel oranges are available winter through spring, but you can find them year-round in some areas.

Valencia Orange

(*Citrus sinensis* (L.) Osbeck)

HISTORICAL BACKGROUND

Some experts believe that the first Valencia oranges were grown in China and brought to Valencia, Spain (where the streets are lined with orange trees). California was the first US region where Valencia oranges were grown, followed by Florida and Texas.

William "Guillermo" Wolfskill was an American pioneer who became a Mexican citizen to own and cultivate land in California while it was still part of Mexico, becoming one of the largest wine producers in the area. In February of 1836, Wolfskill visited the Mission San Gabriel Arcángel, preparing citrus seeds to grow oranges. He was granted possession of land in what would become parking lots and office buildings in Los Angeles. Five years later, Wolfskill planted two acres of citrus with Valencia oranges and a Spanish sweet orange.

In 1842, Wolfskill and his brother, John Reid, bought a large parcel of land in the Sacramento Valley near Winters. He developed the Valencia orange that we know and love today, in honor of the oranges of Valencia, Spain, which it resembles. For all his many contributions to the citrus market, we can call Wolfskill the father of the early citrus of California.

ATTRIBUTES

Valencia oranges are 3 to 4 in [7.5 to 10 cm] in diameter, round to slightly oval. The skin is golden orange and smooth with slight blemishes. Sometimes the fruit absorbs chlorophyll, giving the skin a greenish hue even though the fruit is fully ripe. Valencias are notably easy to peel. Even better, they also have few seeds (1 to 6 per orange), so their juice is rich in flavor without turning bitter after juicing.

THE MANY USES OF VALENCIA ORANGES

Juicing is the best use for this orange. Slicing and topping fish or chicken for grilling also works well, as they do not fall apart like the navel when grilled. Valencia oranges can also be eaten fresh; just keep in mind that unlike with the ubiquitous navel orange, there will be a few seeds.

WHERE THEY GROW

Today, Valencia oranges are grown in California, Florida, and Texas. They're still grown in Spain, and also in Morocco and South Africa.

AVAILABILITY

Valencia oranges are available from February to May.

Cara Cara Orange

(Citrus sinensis (L.) Osbeck)

HISTORICAL BACKGROUND

In 1936, Don Miguel Gimenez Furmeo purchased Hacienda Cara Cara, located in the state of Carabobo, Venezuela. There, for forty years, Don Miguel raised dairy cattle. Because of new farming restrictions, Don Miguel's son sold the cattle and planted a navel orange grove. In 1976, one branch grew brick-red bark and fruit with light pink to red flesh. In 1988, the budwood was sent for testing. The variety was tested for several years and finally approved for cultivation in California and Texas.

ATTRIBUTES

Cara Cara oranges are the same size as navel oranges, with a round to slightly oval shape. The skin is glossy and leathery. The pith is very thin, surrounding red flesh in 8 to 10 segments that are easy to separate. The juice has a high sugar content and a floral and fruity flavor.

THE MANY USES OF CARA CARA ORANGES

Cara Caras are prized for their red flesh and low acidity. Chefs like to use the flesh's rosy hue and the juice's floral character in savory dishes such as chicken, salads, and fish.

WHERE THEY GROW

Cara Cara oranges were first cultivated in Venezuela. Today, they are grown worldwide.

AVAILABILITY

Cara Cara oranges are available from August to October.

Blood Orange

(Citrus sinensis (L.) Osbeck)

HISTORICAL BACKGROUND

In the early nineteenth century on the island of Malta, growers noticed some oranges had splotches of red on the orange skin. The strikingly dark, ruby red flesh and juice within earned them the name blood orange. Seville oranges (similar to the Valencia orange) grafted with pomegranates are the culprit of this fruit.

ATTRIBUTES

Blood oranges are round and range from 2 to 4 in [5 to 10 cm] in diameter. The matte skin can have red blemishes and develops more red on fruit grown in regions with warm days and cool evenings. Blood oranges rarely have seeds, which makes them great for fresh eating as well as juicing. The juice has a bright floral and berry flavor.

THE MANY USES OF BLOOD ORANGES

Blood oranges yield a superb—and delicious—bright red juice. Cooks feature that color in sorbets or sauces. The fruit segments add a pop of color to foods.

WHERE THEY GROW

Today, blood oranges are still grown in Malta, Spain, and Italy. Southern California produces most of the United States' crops.

AVAILABILITY

Blood oranges are plentiful in January and February but can be found in specialty markets from December to July.

Blood Orange-Glazed Carrots

A truly autumnal dish filled with warm-toned colors, the deep red blood oranges and the bright orange carrots with a delectable glossy glaze will be the highlight of the vegetable dishes at any gathering.

2 LB [910 G] CARROTS, PEELED AND
  SLICED ON THE DIAGONAL

½ TSP SALT

½ TSP ORANGE ZEST

2 MEDIUM BLOOD ORANGES, PEELED
  AND SEGMENTED

2 TBSP UNSALTED BUTTER, AT ROOM
  TEMPERATURE

1 TSP FRESH DILL

6 SERVINGS

1. In a medium saucepan, add the carrots and salt with enough water to cover by ½ in [13 mm]. Bring to a boil, lower the heat to a simmer, and cook until tender, 10 to 12 minutes. Drain well.

2. Return the carrots to the pan and add the zest, orange sections, butter, and dill. Toss over low heat until the butter is fully melted and the fruit has broken down to form a glaze, about 5 minutes.

3. Serve immediately. Any leftovers can be cooled completely and stored in a covered container and will keep, refrigerated, for up to a week.

Orange Candied Yams

This easy-to-make side dish is a holiday favorite, guaranteed to complement any meal with its vibrant color and irresistible taste. The yams, coated in a buttery orange syrup, are perfectly balanced in sweet and citrusy flavors.

4 MEDIUM YAMS (ABOUT 2 POUNDS [910 G]), PEELED AND SLICED

1 CUP [240 ML] FRESHLY SQUEEZED ORANGE JUICE

1 TBSP ORANGE ZEST

½ CUP [100 G] GRANULATED SUGAR

½ CUP [100 G] BROWN SUGAR, PACKED

1 TBSP CORNSTARCH

2 TBSP UNSALTED BUTTER, AT ROOM TEMPERATURE, PLUS MORE FOR THE BAKING DISH

MAKES 4 TO 6 SERVINGS

1. Preheat the oven to 300°F [150°C] and butter an oven-proof baking dish.

2. Add the yams to a large saucepan or stock pot and add enough water to cover by ½ in [13 mm]. Bring to a boil, lower the heat to a simmer, and cook until tender, 15 to 20 minutes. Drain well, arrange in the prepared dish, and set aside.

3. In a medium bowl, whisk together the orange juice, zest, sugars, cornstarch, and butter. Pour the mixture over the yams. Bake until the liquid around the yams bubbles, about 1 hour.

4. Serve either hot or cold. Any leftovers can be cooled completely and stored in a covered container and will keep, refrigerated, for up to a week.

Orange Blossom-Glazed Cake

MAKES ONE
9 IN
[23 CM]
ROUND CAKE
(ABOUT 10 TO 12 SERVINGS)

This cake is a sweet ode to the unmistakable sweet fragrance that scents the air when orange trees are in bloom. It's perfect for tea or even brunch or breakfast, when you want something light and sweet, but not too sweet.

CAKE

3 CUPS [420 G] ALL-PURPOSE FLOUR

2 TSP BAKING POWDER

½ TSP SALT

1 CUP [226 G] UNSALTED BUTTER, AT ROOM TEMPERATURE

2 CUPS [400 G] GRANULATED SUGAR

4 LARGE EGGS

1 CUP [240 ML] WHOLE MILK

3 TBSP ORANGE ZEST

CONT'D

TO MAKE THE CAKE

1. Preheat the oven to 350°F [180°C] and spray a 9 in [23 cm] tube pan with nonstick spray.

2. In a large bowl, whisk together the flour, baking powder, and salt and set aside.

3. In the bowl of a stand mixer fitted with the paddle attachment, cream together the butter and sugar on medium speed until fluffy, about 4 minutes. With the mixer running, add the eggs, one at a time, until well incorporated.

4. With the mixer on low speed, add the dry ingredients alternately with the milk, beginning and ending with the dry mixture. Fold in the 3 Tbsp orange zest.

cont'd

GLAZE

⅓ CUP [80 ML] FRESHLY SQUEEZED ORANGE JUICE

¾ CUP [150 G] GRANULATED SUGAR

2 TBSP UNSALTED BUTTER

1 TBSP ORANGE ZEST

5. Pour the batter into the prepared pan and smooth the top evenly. Bake until light brown, 60 to 65 minutes. A cake tester should come out clean when inserted into the center.

6. Set the pan on a rack and let cool for 10 minutes, then invert. Meanwhile, prepare the glaze.

TO MAKE THE GLAZE

7. In a saucepan on medium heat, bring the orange juice, sugar, butter, and zest to a simmer. Pour the hot glaze over the cooled cake. Any leftover glaze should be cooled completely and covered; then it will keep, refrigerated, for up to 1 week, or frozen for up to 2 months.

Orange Hawaiian Muffins

Makes **2 DOZEN MUFFINS**

These light, fluffy muffins are a tropical delight of bright citrus and pineapple. The perfect balance of sweet orange zest and rich, nutty almond flour makes them a delicious indulgence for breakfast or a midday snack.

3½ CUPS [490 G] ALL-PURPOSE FLOUR

1 CUP [120 G] ALMOND FLOUR

2 TSP BAKING POWDER

1 TSP BAKING SODA

1 TSP SEA SALT

3 TBSP ORANGE ZEST

1 CUP [200 G] GRANULATED SUGAR

1 CUP [200 G] BROWN SUGAR, PACKED

4 LARGE EGGS

1 CUP [240 ML] FRESHLY SQUEEZED ORANGE JUICE

⅔ CUP [160 ML] WHOLE MILK

CONT'D

1. Preheat the oven to 400°F [200°C] and line two 12 cup standard muffin pans with paper cups.

2. In a medium bowl, whisk together the flour, almond flour, baking powder, baking soda, and salt. Set aside.

3. In a large bowl, add the orange zest and granulated sugar. With your fingers, rub them together to infuse the oils into the sugar.

4. Add the brown sugar, eggs, juice, milk, and extracts, and whisk together until well blended.

cont'd

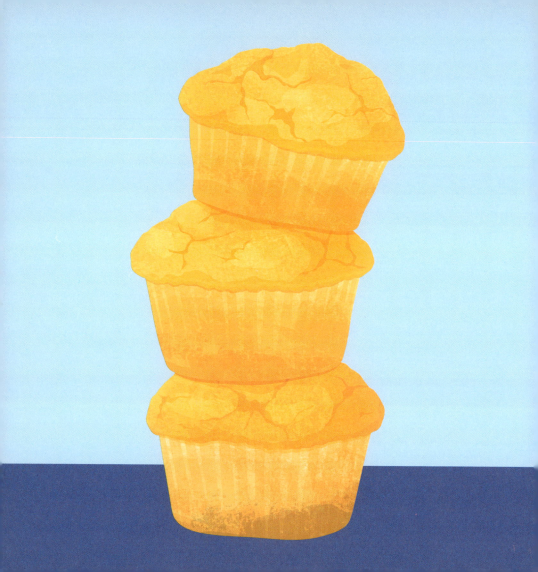

1 TSP VANILLA EXTRACT

1 TSP ALMOND EXTRACT

1 CUP [226 G] UNSALTED BUTTER, MELTED

8 OZ [230 G] CANNED CRUSHED PINEAPPLE, DRAINED

6 OZ [170 G] MACADAMIA NUTS, CHOPPED COARSELY

¼ CUP [50 G] COARSE SUGAR

5. Add the dry ingredients to the sugar-egg mixture, blending until just combined. Stir in the melted butter and mix until smooth. Fold in the pineapple and macadamia nuts.

6. Portion the batter into the muffin cups and top each muffin with a sprinkle of coarse sugar.

7. Bake until a toothpick inserted into the center comes out clean, 15 to 19 minutes. Let cool and serve at room temperature.

The Tick Tock Room's Cara Cara Sticky Rolls

The Tick Tock Room (sometimes called the Tick Tock Tea Room) was a family restaurant in Hollywood from 1930 to 1988, serving hearty foods. These sticky rolls were so popular that they were prepared throughout the day, not only for breakfast. With the essence of citrus, they were also popular for afternoon tea. Sadly, the Tick Tock closed when the next generation wanted out of the business, but you can conjure up that happy atmosphere with these finger-licking treats.

MAKES 18 ROLLS

12 OZ [360 ML] FRESHLY SQUEEZED CARA CARA ORANGE JUICE

½ CUP [100 G] GRANULATED SUGAR

1 CUP [226 G] UNSALTED BUTTER, AT ROOM TEMPERATURE

4 CUPS [560 G] ALL-PURPOSE FLOUR

2 TBSP BAKING POWDER

2 TSP SEA SALT

CONT'D

1. Preheat the oven to 425°F [220°C] and set a rack in the center. Line a 9 by 13 in [23 by 33 cm] baking pan with parchment paper.

2. In a medium saucepan, bring the orange juice to a boil and cook until reduced by half. Add the granulated sugar and ¼ cup [55 g] of the butter and whisk until smooth. Set aside to cool.

3. Melt the remaining ¾ cup [170 g] of butter. Prepare a floured work surface.

cont'd

1⅓ CUPS [315 ML] WHOLE MILK

¼ CUP [50 G] BROWN SUGAR, PACKED

2 TSP FRESH ORANGE ZEST

2 TSP GROUND CINNAMON

¼ TSP GROUND CLOVES

4. In a large bowl, whisk together the flour, baking powder, and salt. Add the milk and the melted butter and mix to form a dough. Knead to combine.

5. Roll out the dough on the floured surface into an 18 by 6 in [46 by 15 cm] rectangle ¼ in [6 mm] thick.

6. In a small bowl, stir together the brown sugar, orange zest, cinnamon, and cloves. Sprinkle the mixture evenly over the dough. Roll up the long side as for cinnamon rolls. Cut into 18 slices.

7. Pour the orange juice mixture into the prepared baking pan. Arrange the rolls, cut-side down, on top of the mixture in a three by six grid.

8. Bake until lightly brown, 20 to 24 minutes. Have ready a serving dish or tray at least 9 by 13 in [23 by 33 cm].

9. As soon as the rolls are done baking, invert the pan onto the serving dish. (If you delay, they will stick to the pan and be hard to remove.) Serve hot, being sure to include some of the sticky glaze.

TANGERINE, TANGELO & MANDARIN

(CITRUS TANGERINA, TANGELO & RETICULATA)

Tangerines, tangelos, and mandarins are all part of the same family, and while they may be small, they are bursting with sweet juice. It can be hard to tell them apart, so ask the most knowledgeable produce staffer. In some areas, the fruits are referred to as clementines. As with most sweet citrus varieties, their flesh and juice can be used somewhat interchangeably in most recipes.

NUTRITIONAL AND HEALTH BENEFITS OF TANGERINES, TANGELOS, AND MANDARINS

Tangerines, tangelos, and mandarins are sweet, small, and perfect fruits to add to any lunch box—for kids and adults alike. For their petite size, they pack a big punch, providing key essential nutrients for added health benefits. They are an excellent source of:

Vitamin C	Magnesium
Potassium	Vitamin A
Calcium	Dietary fiber

Tips on Use

The skin and size of tangerines make them challenging to zest.

There is no need to roll these fruits on a counter, as the skin is soft, and the juice is readily extracted.

Minneola Tangelo

(*Citrus x tangelo*)

HISTORICAL BACKGROUND

The Minneola tangelo (sometimes called a Honeybell) is a hybrid of tangerine and grapefruit. Walter T. Swingle of Eustis, Florida, and Dr. Herbert J. Webber of Riverside, California, created this fruit in 1897, but it was thirty-five years before it was released to the public to grow.

ATTRIBUTES

Minneolas are 3 to 3½ in [7.5 to 9 cm] in diameter, with a slightly elongated neck that gives them a bell shape. The skin is reddish-orange, and they are easy to peel. They're sweet and mildly tart, very juicy, and nearly seedless.

THE MANY USES OF MINNEOLA TANGELOS

Minneola tangelos can be used in any recipe that calls for mandarin oranges. They are perfect for syrups, cakes, cookies, and brownies.

WHERE THEY GROW

Today, Minneola tangelos are cultivated in Southern Florida, Southern California, and Texas.

AVAILABILITY

Minneola tangelos are available from January through April.

Murcott Tangerine

(Citrus reticulata Blanco)

HISTORICAL BACKGROUND

The Murcott tangerine or Delite mandarin is a cross between a tangerine and a sweet orange. Charles Murcott Smith developed the fruit in 1922 using trees he obtained from the USDA in Bayview, Florida. When the trees have a high-bearing year, they produce a much smaller yield the following year.

ATTRIBUTES

Murcott tangerines are small, slightly flattened on both ends, and about 2 in [5 cm] in diameter. The golden-orange peel is slightly textured and easy to remove. The flesh contains up to a dozen tiny seeds.

THE MANY USES OF MURCOTT TANGERINES

The many tiny seeds make the Murcott less desirable for eating out of hand, but the juice is perfect for jam-making, curds, and preserves, and can be frozen to make a refreshing sorbet.

WHERE THEY GROW

Today, the Murcott tangerine is cultivated in Southern California and Florida, though under different names: Murcott Honey in California and Honey in Florida.

AVAILABILITY

Murcott tangerines are available from mid-October through mid-May.

(Ojai) Pixie Mandarin

(*Citrus reticulata* Blanco)

HISTORICAL BACKGROUND

Howard B. Frost of the University of California, Riverside, obtained the parent seed for the Pixie in 1927, testing and developing it over many years by planting and growing trees in various climates. The experimentation took so long because the trees can take up to four years to produce their first harvest, and another four to bear fruitfully.

After thirty-eight years, in 1965, university breeders Robert Soost and James Cameron released the Pixie and suggested it be grown as backyard fruit. In the 1980s, Soost and Cameron contacted Frank Noyes of Ojai to test their new mandarin. He declared it a perfect, seedless, delicious fruit. As of this writing, there are over twenty-five thousand Ojai Pixie trees growing on fifty-two family farms.

ATTRIBUTES

Ojai Pixies are 2 to 3 in [5 to 7.5 cm] in diameter. Sold in 1 lb [455 g] mesh bags (each with five or six fruits), these delightful miniature fruits are irresistible to children; even the youngest can peel them easily.

THE MANY USES OF PIXIE MANDARINS

Pixies are popular for peeling and eating out of hand, but you can easily segment them to top a salad.

WHERE THEY GROW

Today, Pixies are grown only in the Ojai Valley close to Santa Barbara, California.

AVAILABILITY

Pixies are available from March to June.

Temecula Sweet Tangerine

(Citrus reticulata)

HISTORICAL BACKGROUND

In the 1980s, C. T. Lin crossed a Satsuma and a Ponkan tangerine in his Montana hothouse. Eleven years later, Lin moved to Temecula, California, an agricultural area between San Diego and Riverside known for producing wine and fresh produce. There he planted his first trees for the tangerines that he named Temecula Sweets. He later sold half of his 24-acre grove to retired airline pilot Norm Jones. To this day, Jones is still harvesting there.

ATTRIBUTES

The Temecula Sweet is about 3 in [7.5 cm] in diameter. It earned its unfortunate nickname, "the ugly tangerine," from the peel's shriveled appearance. You can shake it to loosen the segments within for even easier peeling.

THE MANY USES OF TEMECULA SWEETS

The firm segments lend themselves to dipping in chocolate for a simple dessert or scattering on top of a salad. Blended with yogurt into a smoothie, the fruit makes a refreshing pick-me-up drink.

WHERE THEY GROW

Temecula Sweets are cultivated in just the one location, in a 24-acre grove along the Santa Margarita River in Temecula.

AVAILABILITY

Temecula Sweets are available from late winter through the spring months.

Caribbean Black Bean Mandarin Salad

This refreshing salad blends the earthy richness of black beans with the sweet tang of mandarin oranges. Perfect for a light lunch or as a zesty side dish, it brings the flavors of the tropics to your table!

3 TBSP RED WINE VINEGAR

1 TSP OLIVE OIL

1 TSP DIJON MUSTARD

¼ CUP [10 G] MINCED FRESH CILANTRO

¼ TSP GROUND CUMIN

¼ TSP FRESHLY GROUND BLACK PEPPER

¼ MEDIUM RED ONION, CHOPPED

2 GARLIC CLOVES, MINCED

4 SMALL MANDARIN ORANGES,
   3 SEGMENTED AND 1 JUICED

ONE 15 OZ [425 G] CAN BLACK BEANS,
   DRAINED AND RINSED

RICE OR SHREDDED LETTUCE, FOR
   SERVING

1. In a large bowl, whisk together the vinegar, oil, mustard, cilantro, cumin, pepper, onion, garlic, and the juice of 1 mandarin until blended.

2. Add the mandarin segments and black beans. Toss to coat thoroughly.

3. Serve on a bed of rice or shredded lettuce.

SERVES 4

Bullocks Wilshire's Mandarin Chicken Salad

SERVES 8

Bullocks Wilshire was an upscale department store where shoppers could—and commonly did—spend an entire day. The tearoom featured fashion shows while guests dined on salads and finger sandwiches. This salad was one of the store's most popular dishes.

SALAD

1 HEAD ICEBERG LETTUCE, CHOPPED

3 CUPS [710 G] DICED COOKED CHICKEN

4 SMALL MANDARIN ORANGES, PEELED AND SEGMENTED

4 OZ [115 G] ALMONDS, SLICED AND TOASTED

CANOLA OIL, FOR FRYING

ONE 6.75 OZ [190 G] PACKAGE WONTON WRAPPERS, SLICED INTO STRIPS

CONT'D

TO MAKE THE SALAD

1. In a large bowl, combine the lettuce, chicken, mandarin segments, and almonds. Set aside.

2. In a saucepan, heat 1½ in [4 cm] of oil to 370°F [188°C]. Line a plate with paper towels. Fry the wonton wrappers until golden brown and puffy, about 1 to 2 minutes. Transfer to the paper towels.

cont'd

MUSTARD MAYONNAISE DRESSING

1 CUP [240 G] MAYONNAISE

2 TSP PREPARED MUSTARD

1 TSP SOY SAUCE

1 TSP CANOLA OR OTHER NEUTRAL VEGETABLE OIL

¾ TSP WORCESTERSHIRE SAUCE

¼ CUP [60 ML] FRESHLY SQUEEZED MANDARIN ORANGE JUICE

TO MAKE THE DRESSING

3. While the wonton wrappers cool, make the dressing: In a medium bowl, whisk together the mayonnaise, mustard, soy sauce, canola oil, Worcestershire sauce, and juice until smooth.

4. Drizzle ¾ cup [180 ml] of dressing over the salad. With two forks or salad tongs, toss the salad. Crumble the wonton wrappers into bite-size shards over the salad and serve immediately.

5. Leftover dressing will keep, refrigerated in an airtight container, for up to 2 weeks.

Panko-Crusted Shrimp with Mandarin Sauce

Makes **8 APPETIZER SERVINGS** *or* **2 MAIN DISH SERVINGS**

These flavorful shrimp are served in many tiki bars from coast to coast. Enjoy them with a tropical drink, and you will feel like you are in the islands.

PANKO SHRIMP

½ CUP [70 G] ALL-PURPOSE FLOUR

1¼ TSP SEASONED PEPPER

2 LARGE EGGS

1½ CUPS [125 G] PANKO

1 LB [455 G] JUMBO SHRIMP (16–20 SIZE), RAW, THAWED, AND SHELLED, RETAINING THE TAILS

CANOLA OIL, FOR FRYING

CONT'D

TO MAKE THE SHRIMP

1. In a large bowl, combine the flour and 1 tsp of the seasoned pepper and set aside.

2. In a medium bowl, whisk together the eggs and 1 Tbsp of water until frothy and set aside.

3. In a medium shallow bowl, mix the panko and the remaining ¼ tsp seasoned pepper.

4. Dip each shrimp first in the flour, then the egg mixture, and then the panko, coating both sides. Place on a dish until all of the shrimp have been coated.

cont'd

MANDARIN SAUCE

½ CUP [120 ML] SOY SAUCE

1 TBSP SESAME OIL

3 SMALL MANDARINS, JUICED (ABOUT 1 CUP [240 ML])

¼ CUP [50 G] BROWN SUGAR

3 TBSP CORNSTARCH WHISKED INTO ¼ CUP [60 ML] WATER

2 TSP MANDARIN ZEST

5. Heat 1½ in [4 cm] of oil in a deep-frying pan to 350°F [180°C]. Line a baking sheet with paper towels. Use a thermometer to ensure that the temperature remains steady as each batch is fried.

6. Add the coated shrimp to the oil in batches, taking care not to overcrowd the pan. Fry until lightly brown, 2½ to 3 minutes. Drain on the paper towels.

TO MAKE THE SAUCE

7. Whisk together the soy sauce, sesame oil, mandarin juice, brown sugar, and diluted cornstarch in a saucepan until smooth.

8. Heat on low, whisking until thickened, 3 to 4 minutes. Whisk in the zest. Serve alongside the shrimps for dipping.

Pineapple-Tangerine Glazed Yams

Makes **6** servings

These fruit-glazed yams are a tropical twist on a classic side dish. The sweet and tangy glaze, enlivened with cinnamon, complements the natural richness of the yams, creating a vibrant and flavorful dish perfect for the winter holiday season.

1 MEDIUM PAPAYA, CUT INTO CHUNKS

8 OZ [230 G] CRUSHED PINEAPPLE, DRAINED AND JUICE RESERVED

3 MEDIUM TANGERINES, PEELED AND SEGMENTED

3 TO 4 LB [1.4 TO 1.8 KG] YAMS, COOKED, PEELED, AND SLICED INTO ¼ IN [6 MM] PIECES

½ CUP [120 ML] FRESHLY SQUEEZED MANDARIN JUICE

1 TBSP CORNSTARCH

¼ TSP SEA SALT

1 DASH GROUND WHITE PEPPER

1 DASH GROUND CINNAMON

1 TBSP UNSALTED BUTTER, CUT INTO 4 PIECES

1. Preheat the oven to 350°F [180°C].

2. Place the papaya, pineapple, tangerines, and yams in a 9 by 13 in [23 by 33 cm] casserole dish and set aside.

3. In a saucepan over medium heat, whisk together the reserved pineapple juice and mandarin juice with the cornstarch, salt, pepper, and cinnamon until thickened, about 8 minutes.

4. Pour the mixture over the fruit and dot with the butter.

5. Cover with foil and bake for 10 minutes. Serve hot. Cool completely before storing in a covered container. It will keep, refrigerated, for up to a week.

Tangerine Maple Barbecue Spareribs

You can prepare spareribs even in the winter months in your oven. Try these tangy, sweet, and spicy ribs smothered in a delicious tangerine-based barbecue sauce—a pop of summer, all year long.

½ CUP [120 ML] FRESHLY SQUEEZED TANGERINE JUICE

½ CUP [120 ML] SOY SAUCE

½ CUP [120 ML] MAPLE SYRUP

¼ CUP [85 G] HONEY

2 TBSP DRY MUSTARD POWDER

2 RACKS SPARERIBS, MEMBRANE REMOVED

1. Preheat the oven to 400°F [200°C].

2. In a small saucepan, bring the tangerine juice to a boil, then simmer, stirring occasionally, until reduced by half, about 5 minutes. Set aside.

3. Add the soy sauce, maple syrup, honey, and mustard powder and simmer for about 3 minutes.

4. Line a baking sheet with thick foil. Place the ribs on the foil and brush with sauce on both sides.

5. Wrap foil around the ribs and seal all the edges. Bake until the ribs are tender and about to fall off the bone, about 1 hour. The ribs will keep in an airtight container in the refrigerator for up to 1 week.

2 RACKS OF RIBS
(4 servings)

Chocolate Fudge Cake with Fresh Tangelo Icing

MAKES ONE
8 IN
[20 CM]
ROUND
CAKE
(ABOUT 12 SERVINGS)

This rich, indulgent two-layer chocolate cake is topped with a refreshing tangelo icing, perfectly balancing sweet and citrusy flavors.

CAKE

2 CUPS [240 G] CAKE FLOUR

6 TBSP [30 G] DUTCH COCOA POWDER

1 TSP BAKING SODA

½ TSP SEA SALT

½ CUP [113 G] UNSALTED BUTTER, AT ROOM TEMPERATURE

1¼ CUPS [250 G] GRANULATED SUGAR

1 TSP VANILLA EXTRACT

2 LARGE EGGS, AT ROOM TEMPERATURE

1 CUP [240 ML] WHOLE MILK

CONT'D

TO MAKE THE CAKE

1. Preheat the oven to 350°F [180°C]. Spray two 8 in [20 cm] round cake pans with nonstick spray.

2. In a medium bowl, whisk together the cake flour, cocoa powder, baking soda, and salt. Set aside.

3. In the bowl of a stand mixer with the paddle attachment on medium speed, cream together the butter and sugar until light and fluffy, about 3 minutes. Scrape down the sides with a rubber spatula. Add the vanilla and eggs and blend until completely incorporated.

cont'd

TANGELO ICING

⅓ CUP [45 G] DRY MILK POWDER

2 TBSP FRESHLY SQUEEZED TANGELO JUICE

2 TBSP FRESHLY SQUEEZED LEMON JUICE

3 CUPS [360 G] CONFECTIONERS' SUGAR

1 LARGE EGG WHITE

½ CUP [90 G] VEGETABLE SHORTENING

¼ CUP [55 G] UNSALTED BUTTER, AT ROOM TEMPERATURE

⅛ TSP SALT

1 TBSP TANGELO ZEST

4. Add the dry mixture alternately with the milk, beginning and ending with the dry mixture and blending after each addition.

5. Divide the batter into the prepared cake pans and smooth to even the tops. Bake until a toothpick inserted into the center comes out clean, 35 to 40 minutes. Cool in the pans for 10 minutes, then invert onto a rack to cool completely, 2 to 3 hours.

6. When completely cooled, wrap the layers individually first with plastic wrap and then with foil. Freeze for 8 to 10 hours.

7. The cake is easiest to ice when just out of the freezer.

TO MAKE THE TANGELO ICING

8. In the bowl of a stand mixer with the whip attachment, dissolve the dry milk powder in the juices and add the sugar and egg white. Starting at low speed and gradually increasing to high speed, whip until thick, about 5 minutes.

9. Change to the paddle attachment. With the mixer running at medium speed, add chunks of the shortening and butter and blend until fluffy, about 5 minutes. Stir in the salt and zest.

10. Remove the cake from the freezer and frost with the icing while the cake is still frozen. After icing, allow the cake to thaw and serve.

11. Store covered at room temperature or refrigerated.

> NOTE If you prepare the icing ahead of serving; do not refrigerate, as it will harden. Cover and store at room temperature until needed.

BUDDHA'S HAND & CITRON

Buddha's hand citrus is one of the most exotic-looking fruits and one of the most symbolic in Asian culture. Together with the singular citron, they form the odd couple of the citrus family.

NUTRITIONAL AND HEALTH BENEFITS OF BUDDHA'S HAND AND CITRON

Buddha's hands and citrons are traditionally used in medical practices and aromatherapy to relieve pain, soothe coughing and digestive distress, lower blood pressure, and aid in skin healing.

Buddha's hands and citrons are an excellent source of:

Vitamin C

Antioxidants

Tips on Use

The Buddha's hand can be zested to extract the oils and zest from the surface of the fruit.

The citron's pith (not the skin) is the part most commonly used. Cut through the peel to the pith and cut the pith into smaller pieces.

Buddha's Hand

(Citrus medica var. sarcodactylis)

Also known as the fingered citron, Buddha's hands are the oddballs of the citrus family.

HISTORICAL BACKGROUND

The Buddha's hand is native to Asia; after its discovery, as early as 300 BCE, it was planted throughout the Mediterranean. In the late nineteenth century the Buddha's hand was brought from Japan to California.

ATTRIBUTES

Buddha's hands are the bright yellow of lemons but with many fingers, resembling an octopus or squid with flowing tentacles. One of the simplest ways to use this citrus is to slice the "fingers" to release the deep citrus aroma and flavor into a dish.

THE MANY USES OF BUDDHA'S HANDS

Large fingers of the fruit can be sliced and submerged in vodka, olive oil, or sugar to infuse them with its pungent aroma. You can also infuse the fruit into tea to aid immune response and healing when you feel a cold or flu coming on.

WHERE THEY GROW

Today, the Buddha's hand is cultivated primarily in East Asia, specifically in Guangdong and Fujian provinces. In recent years, Southern California has begun growing it to meet the demand from American home cooks and chefs.

AVAILABILITY

Buddha's hand has one of the briefest harvest seasons of all citrus, lasting only six weeks, from late November through December.

Citron
(Citrus medica)

HISTORICAL BACKGROUND

Citron is the oldest variety of the citrus family; seeds recovered in excavation areas of the Middle East have been dated from over 700 to 500 BCE. The Latin name, *Citrus medica*, refers to the former state of Media, now Iran.

ATTRIBUTES

Citrons look much like a standard lemon, but with very rough-textured skin. The peel is thick, mostly pith, and the flesh is light in juice.

THE MANY USES OF CITRONS

Citron is valued mainly for its peel and oils. It is not eaten like a lemon or orange, but is used in candies, jams, preserves, and infused drinks. The candied peel is used in cookies, quick breads, and fruitcake, especially for religious holidays and celebrations. The essential oils extracted from the citron are some of the most fragrant used in aromatherapy and perfumery.

WHERE THEY GROW

Citron trees flourish in the warm coastal climate of their native Mediterranean. Today, they are cultivated on the smaller coastal islands of Greece, France, and Italy.

AVAILABILITY

Citrons are typically available from September to March, with periods of unavailability depending on the weather.

Buddha's Hand Shortbread Sugar Cookies

Citrus and buttery, rich shortbread are a match made in heaven. Here the lemony tang of the Buddha's hand and the creamy, crunchy texture of the shortbread make an irresistible combination—rest assured, you can't eat just one.

1¼ CUPS [280 G] UNSALTED BUTTER, AT ROOM TEMPERATURE

¾ CUP [150 G] GRANULATED SUGAR

¾ TSP SEA SALT

⅓ CUP [240 G] BUDDHA'S HAND FINGERS, FINELY CHOPPED

3¾ CUPS [525 G] ALL-PURPOSE FLOUR

⅓ CUP [65 G] COARSE SUGAR

6 OZ [170 G] SEMISWEET CHOCOLATE, MELTED AND COOLED

1. Preheat the oven to 325°F [165°C]. Line two baking sheets with parchment paper.

2. In the bowl of a stand mixer with the paddle attachment on medium speed, cream together the butter, sugar, salt, and chopped Buddha's hand until fluffy, about 10 minutes.

3. Add the flour and stir in by hand, not with the mixer, until completely incorporated.

cont'd

4. Divide the dough in half and turn each half out onto a prepared baking sheet. Roll each half out into a rectangle about ½ in [13 mm] thick; do not try to cover the entire baking sheet. Sprinkle evenly with the coarse sugar and press the sugar into the dough with your hands. Cut the dough into squares or diamonds, about 3 in [7.5 cm], and separate them on the baking sheet. They won't spread, so they can be fairly close together, with just enough space for heat circulation.

5. Bake until the cookies turn golden, 20 to 25 minutes. Cool on a rack. Dip half of each cookie into the melted chocolate. Place back on the baking sheets and let rest until thoroughly cooled. They will keep in a covered container for up to 1 week.

Candied Citron Fruitcake

MAKES 3 LOAF CAKES

When traveling in Italy during the holidays, you will find candied citrons everywhere in the markets. This cake is an ode to their delicious, sweet-tart bite.

If you can't locate citron fruit, you can certainly use the readily available packaged candied citron. But if you can get your hands on the fresh fruit, the result is well worth the time and patience you'll invest in making your own.

2 LB [910 G] CANDIED CITRON (RECIPE FOLLOWS, OR USE STORE-BOUGHT)

1 LB [455 G] CANDIED CHERRIES

1 CUP [240 ML] ORANGE LIQUEUR (TRIPLE SEC, GRAND MARNIER, OR COINTREAU)

5 TBSP [75 G] UNSALTED BUTTER, AT ROOM TEMPERATURE

6 TBSP [90 G] GRANULATED SUGAR

CONT'D

1. In a large bowl, combine the citron and cherries with the orange liqueur and toss to coat. Cover and refrigerate for a week, stirring every few days.

2. Preheat the oven to 350°F [180°C]. Spray three 1 lb [455 g] loaf pans with nonstick spray.

cont'd

½ CUP [100 G] BROWN SUGAR, PACKED

3 LARGE EGGS

¼ CUP [60 ML] ORANGE HONEY

1 TSP VANILLA EXTRACT

PINCH OF SALT

1⅓ CUPS [160 G] ALL-PURPOSE FLOUR

1 CUP [120 G] PECAN HALVES

3. In the bowl of a stand mixer with the paddle attachment, cream together the butter and sugars on medium speed until smooth. Add the eggs, honey, vanilla, and salt, and mix until smooth.

4. Fold in the flour, pecans, and fruit with the soaking liqueur by hand.

5. Divide the mixture into the prepared loaf pans. Bake until a toothpick inserted in the center comes out clean, about 40 minutes.

6. Cool in pans for 10 minutes before cooling on a rack. Store wrapped in plastic wrap after cooled completely for up to a week. To freeze, wrap in foil over the plastic wrap for up to a month.

Candied Citron Peel

12 LARGE CITRONS

4 CUPS [800 G] GRANULATED SUGAR

1. Cut each citron in half and scoop out the flesh with a spoon. Place the peels in a large pot and cover with room-temperature water. Bring to a full boil and boil for 3 minutes. Drain.

2. Return the citron peels to the large pot, cover with water, and boil for 3 more minutes. Drain and repeat once more, this time not draining the water.

3. Let rest for 1 hour, then cover with water and bring back to a boil for 5 minutes, rest for 1 hour, and repeat the boiling one last time, or repeat until the peels are tender and translucent.

4. Meanwhile, line a rimmed baking sheet with parchment paper.

5. Drain the peels with a slotted spoon and arrange on the parchment paper. When the peels are cool enough to handle, cut into ½ in [13 mm] strips. Toss them with sugar, spreading them out to give the peels room. Let dry, uncovered, for 24 hours. If they are sticky, toss them with more sugar. Let them dry for two more days. Store until ready to use.

6. Store in a tightly sealed container for up to 3 weeks. If you store the peels before they are dried, you may get mold.

MAKES ABOUT **4 POUNDS** [1.8 kg], depending on the size of the citrons

Buddha's Hand Vodka Martini

Aromatic and zesty, this martini highlights the striking citrus flavor of Buddha's hand with a crisp, refined finish.

3 OZ [90 ML] BUDDHA'S HAND VODKA (RECIPE FOLLOWS)

½ OZ [15 ML] DRY VERMOUTH

1 OLIVE, LEMON TWIST, OR A FINGER OF BUDDHA'S HAND

1. Fill a cocktail shaker with ice and Buddha's Hand Vodka. Shake vigorously 20 times.

2. Coat a cold martini glass with the vermouth and shake out any excess. Strain in the vodka. Top with an olive, lemon twist, or a finger of Buddha's hand.

MAKES ONE DRINK

Buddha's Hand Vodka

ONE 750 ML BOTTLE GOOD-QUALITY VODKA

1 BUDDHA'S HAND

1. Pour out 1½ cups [360 ml] of vodka into a glass container and save for another use.

2. Cut the fingers off the Buddha's hand and if needed, cut small enough to fit into the vodka bottle. Submerge them in the vodka. If you run out of room, pour out more vodka.

3. Place the cap back on the bottle, seal tightly, and store in a cool, dark place. Every few days, give the vodka a swirl to infuse it with the citrus oils.

4. The vodka will be ready to be enjoyed in 60 days. It will keep indefinitely.

MAKES 390 ML

MIXING UP FRUITS:
HYBRIDS

All modern-day, familiar citrus fruits are hybrids of four original historical fruits. Meet the ancestors of those common fruits we eat daily:

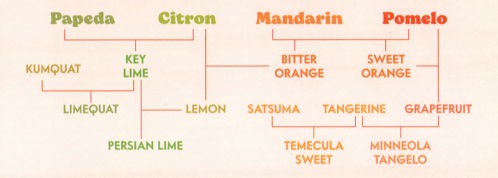

Papeda   **Citron**   **Mandarin**   **Pomelo**

KUMQUAT   KEY LIME   BITTER ORANGE   SWEET ORANGE

LIMEQUAT   LEMON   SATSUMA   TANGERINE   GRAPEFRUIT

PERSIAN LIME   TEMECULA SWEET   MINNEOLA TANGELO

In your own way, you can be a hybridizer in your cooking. Combining citrus varieties in cooking and baking adds unique flavors to your culinary repertoire. When using tart fruit, you sometimes need to balance it with a sweet variety.

Four Citrus Ambrosia Salad

Though calling this "salad" might be a bit of a stretch in the modern sense of the word, ambrosia salad is a deeply traditional church potluck dish hailing from the South. Today there are many variations available. My sister Pattie considers a holiday spread complete only if this salad is on the table.

1 LARGE ORANGE, SEGMENTED

2 SMALL TANGERINES, SEGMENTED

1 LARGE GRAPEFRUIT, SEGMENTED

1 SMALL MEYER LEMON, SEGMENTED

1 CUP [240 G] SOUR CREAM OR VANILLA YOGURT

1¼ CUPS [54 G] MINI MARSHMALLOWS

1 CUP [256 G] CANNED CRUSHED PINEAPPLE, DRAINED

1½ CUPS [150 G] SWEETENED FLAKED COCONUT

1. In a large bowl, combine the orange, tangerine, grapefruit, and lemon segments. Fold in the sour cream, marshmallows, pineapple, and coconut.

2. Transfer the salad to a covered bowl and refrigerate for at least 2 hours before serving.

3. For a festive look, decorate with additional citrus segments.

LLT (Lemon, Lime, Tangerine) Vinaigrette

MAKES
1 CUP [240 ML]

If you've got citrus on hand, you will never need to buy a store-bought vinaigrette again. Grab a bowl and whisk, or even a coffee mug and a fork, and you'll have a restaurant-worthy dressing on hand for days to come.

¼ CUP [60 ML] WHITE WINE VINEGAR

1 TSP DIJON MUSTARD

1 TSP TANGERINE ZEST

1 TSP LEMON ZEST

½ TSP LIME ZEST

⅔ CUP [160 ML] CANOLA OIL

¼ CUP [30 G] PINE NUTS, TOASTED AND CHOPPED

1. In a small bowl, vigorously whisk together the vinegar, mustard, and zests.

2. While continuing to whisk, pour in the oil in a steady stream, whisking until the mixture emulsifies.

3. Stir in the pine nuts. Use to dress your salad greens.

4. The salad dressing will keep in a sealed jar or bottle, refrigerated, for up to 2 weeks. Before using, shake vigorously.

Chocolate-Dipped Triple Citrus Cookies

The contrasting, distinctive blend of three different citrus flavors with the creamy chocolate offers up a delicious sweet treat for any occasion.

¾ CUP [170 G] UNSALTED BUTTER, AT ROOM TEMPERATURE

½ CUP [100 G] GRANULATED SUGAR

2 CUPS [280 G] ALL-PURPOSE FLOUR

1 TBSP ORANGE ZEST

1 TBSP LEMON ZEST

1 TSP LIME ZEST

6 OZ [170 G] SEMISWEET CHOCOLATE, MELTED AND COOLED BUT KEPT LIQUID OVER WARM WATER

Makes about 2 DOZEN COOKIES

1. Preheat the oven to 350°F [180°C]. Line two baking sheets with parchment paper.

2. In the bowl of a stand mixer with the paddle attachment, blend the butter on low speed until creamy. Add the sugar and increase the speed to medium. Beat until fluffy, about 5 minutes.

3. Add the flour and mix until well blended. Fold in the zests by hand.

4. Scoop the dough with a size #70 cookie scoop onto one of the prepared baking sheets. Flatten each scoop with the palm of your hand.

5. Bake until light brown, 18 to 20 minutes. Cool completely on a wire rack.

6. Dip each cooled cookie halfway into the melted chocolate and cool on the clean parchment-lined baking sheet.

Recipe Directory

Acknowledgments

Putting a book together is not that different from the realities of owning a restaurant, in that you never get to meet or thank many people behind the scenes. So I hope that you forgive me if I neglect to thank you.

My family and friends: Neil, my partner in life for over forty years and husband for as long as it's been legal, has put up with all the side trips and listened to me talk about my love of citrus. I love to point out the "Happy Trees" filled with oranges as he rolls his eyes.

To my late father, George Geary, for instilling in me my values, and my number one girl, Mom (Patti), for always being on the other end of the phone daily to listen to my dreams and problems and to share our Southern California sunsets. Monica and Pattie, my two sisters, are two roses alongside this thorn. Jonathan, thank you for being a great friend. Trina Kaye is the number one publicist ever.

Thank you to the three news families I work with regularly—FOX5 (KSWB) San Diego, WGN Midday News, and NBC Tampa WFLA Daytime—and all the stations coast to coast that have promoted all my books. And to Tiffany Frowiss, my number one producer for fifteen years.

Thank you to Robert Schueller at Melissa's World Variety Produce for shipping out citrus at a moment's notice, and to the California Citrus State Historic Park, for keeping the historical values and history of the industry alive.

Thank you Rebecca Hollingsworth for the beautiful artwork in this book.

Lastly, to the whole team at Chronicle Books: From the design team to my editorial supporters, Sarah Billingsley, Dena Rayess, Alex Galou, and Kristi Hein: Thank you for believing in my work and love for the citrus industry. This team is the best in publishing, creating magic with my words like no other.

ABOUT GEORGE GEARY

Citrus, Illustrated is George's seventeenth book. George is known for creating iconic foods for the Walt Disney Company, where he was the award-winning pastry chef for ten years, and for food on TV shows, such as the cheesecakes on the hit show *The Golden Girls*. George is a sought-after speaker on legendary and landmark Hollywood restaurants.